GUILTY STAINS

From Pain to Deliverance:
How *HE* Erased the Stains

This book is a work of non-fiction. Names, characters, businesses, organizations, places, events and incidents are the product of the author's life.

For information, contact the author at www.fluiditycontentwriting.com.

Book and Cover design by XCel Creative Solutions

Editing services provided by TruThink Publishing

ISBN: 978-0-692-14314-8

First Edition: October 2018

10 9 8 7 6 5 4 3 2 1

This book is dedicated to all those who, at one point in their lives, have felt the stains of their pain or who are living in the shadows of their stains. You, my dear, are enough... **actually, you are more than enough** *and my prayer is that you write your own love letter and become the shining star* **GOD** *intended you to be.*

"Guilt is the worst demon to bear, strangling you from the inside of your body.

Apologize.

Make amends.

Let go.

Breathe free."

~ Nikita Gill

Contents

GUILTY STAINS

is a labor of love that was borne out of pain, endurance, trust, love and truth ...

PREFACE

For so long, I lived my life in a defeated mindset, conjuring up images of a life I wished I had, but more than that, doing my best to live out the fantasy in a world that truly became make-believe. The problem with make-believe and fantasy is that at some inconvenient point, the truth comes to life. It becomes painfully clear, and suddenly, the picture of truth is not as pretty as the deceit of the fantasies. That sounds like a conundrum, I know, but that statement was my reality for a very long time. I didn't want to remember the molestation, divorce, being evicted from our home as a little girl, feeling unloved and rejected time and time again, not being chosen and worst of all, betrayal by the woman who gave me life.

God tried to get my attention for a very long time and for a very long time, I ignored the fact that this book would come to fruition. One way or another, I had to face the truth, live it, breath it, as much as it hurt. I contemplated how much truth would affect the lives of so many. Keeping the truth, the dirty little secrets and guarding them with my being seemed like the better option; not for me, but for the ones who hurt me most. When I mentioned writing this book to a sibling, her first thought was the same as mine. She wanted to let sleeping

1

dogs lie because that way they couldn't come back to bite us. It wasn't "us" who would be affected because I had to watch that sleeping dog lie there, comfortable as he was, while I experienced the stench and was bitten by the fleas meant for him. The longer I waited to finish writing, the more I was bitten.

What I have learned most about telling my story in my own way, is that there will always be people who will be willing to walk away from you if your purpose doesn't serve theirs. You must walk on anyway. Those who choose to stay will stay and will hold fast and tighter the tougher the battle becomes. Those are the warriors meant to go the distance with you. I've held on to my warriors tightly, never looking back. Most times in this life, family will be the ones to hurt you more than anyone else ever could. The old saying, "familiarity breeds contempt," could never ring truer.

One morning on my drive to work, listening to Joel Osteen's inspirational message, *God Remembers*, it hit me. This defeated mindset could no longer reside in the crevices of my life. It wasn't that God hadn't graced me with everything I needed to live an abundant life, but I had chosen to *pretend* that life was real instead of living and breathing *in* that reality. That seemed so much easier until this particular morning. No longer could I pretend to have things that I didn't; work in a job that I didn't; believe things I really didn't; or see things I really couldn't. No, this particular morning caused the deceit to look ugly, blemished, and though the truth came and sat on my shoulders, it wasn't the burden I felt it would be to carry all those years ago. Instead, the burdens of deceit and fallacy I had been carrying for so many years lifted like a mirage. It was as though they never existed, but they still carried meaning in my new truth. My new truth is a much lighter load to carry. Every now and again, I look over my shoulder and remind myself I am unique, and God created me to do something in this life that no one else can do. Nobody but my truth and me.

As you thumb through the pages of this book, know that its intent is to bring healing not hurt, light not darkness, and love not hate. As I was writing a portion of this book one morning, one of my sisters sent a message to my mother, my sisters and me. The message read in part: "... this scripture has been in my heart for quite some time to share with you. Today, I'm being obedient. I would like you all to read and pray with me that God speaks to our hearts and minds. We will not be defeated in Jesus name." The scripture reads, *4 "Love is patient, love is kind. It does not envy, it does not boast, it is not proud. 5It does not dishonor others, it is not self-seeking, it is not easily angered, it keeps no record of wrongs. 6Love does not delight in evil but rejoices with the truth. 7It always protects, always trusts, always hopes, always perseveres" (1 Corinthians 13:4-7).*

Consequently, we own our own truths, but what we do not own is how others may perceive our truth. We can choose to heal or continue hurting. Either way, the choice is ours unless we relinquish that choice to someone else. My choice(s) and my voice have been taken away from me for far too long. The time is now to reclaim it in the most authentic, genuine and loving way I know how. This book is the vehicle God has given me, and I must drive forward. What I know for sure is if we focus on the mess for too long, we will miss the message. I believe this body of work has a message so profound that it will be like spring water flowing freely in the middle of a desert for some who have trod in very similar footsteps as I for far too long. Still, others will relate because they understand the impact these stains have had on family members, friends, or loved ones.

Unfortunately, so often in the African-American community, we protect the perpetrator while the victim continues to suffer in silence. I never understood why we as a community choose to look the other way and strive so hard to keep dirty little secrets that eventually become enormous boulders. I will also never understand why the impact of my story and stories like mine are looked upon as betrayal, but the very acts committed against me (and others like me) are so worthy of protecting. We lock arms protecting secrets, perhaps not realizing those secrets tear down; they very rarely uplift. That is why they are secrets, but unearthing secrets empowers the victim into becoming her best self and into the realization that she is a victor, more than a conqueror.

Romans 8:31-39 says, [31]"What, then, shall we say in response to these things? If God is for us, who can be against us? [32] He who did not spare his own Son, but gave him up for us all—how will he not also, along with him, graciously give us all things? [33] Who will bring any charge against those whom God has chosen? It is God who justifies. [34] Who then is the one who condemns? No one. Christ Jesus who died—more than that, who was raised to life—is at the right hand of God and is also interceding for us. [35] Who shall separate us from the love of Christ? Shall trouble or hardship or persecution or famine or nakedness or danger or sword? [36] As it is written:

"For your sake we face death all day long; we are considered as sheep to be slaughtered."[a]

[37]No, in all these things we are more than conquerors through him who loved us. [38] For I am convinced that neither death nor life, neither angels nor demons,[b] neither the present nor the future, nor any powers,[39] neither height nor depth, nor anything else in all creation, will be able to separate us from the love of God that is in Christ Jesus our Lord."

What was meant to destroy has brought strength, wisdom and clarity. My family is like yours, and there's a dollop of dysfunction, stirred together with heartbreak and unspeakable pain. Throughout this book, the pain of it all now speaks with purpose. The purpose has taken her rightful place amongst the pain rising from the depths into the heights of the highest highs.

I vacillated many times over whether I should continue writing this book or write it if only to allow it to be therapeutic for me, writing it out of me but keeping it to myself. I decided that wasn't therapy at all. I tried to talk myself out of sharing my story with anyone for fear it would hurt my family. Many of my family members wished for me to only tell certain parts of my story, while leaving out others to protect those who caused me harm. In many ways, I still felt as if I was being stained with guilt because I no longer wanted to sit with them in silence. Consequently, I figured if I wasn't going to tell the whole truth, then I may as well leave the half-truths to those who wanted to tell them. I gave them the choice that wasn't afforded to me.

So, I moved forward, empowered by a movement I could not have known was coming. Yes, that movement, the #MeToo movement. This movement confirmed for me I was doing the right thing at the right time and in the right space. I began writing this book long before this movement, but as I began to delve deeper and deeper into the abyss that was my childhood, the demons, the ghosts chased me down. I was out of breath from being chased. I knew I could eliminate the chase by putting my pen down, at least for a time, but once the dust of the moment settled, I knew the darkness would find me. That just didn't seem right. And so, out of the depths of my pain arises this work of art.

Guilty Stains is a labor of love borne out of pain, endurance, trust, love and truth, and not necessarily in that particular order. Each chapter represents a stain that shaped and reshaped my life in a way that I never could have imagined. I couldn't write this book without also sharing with you how the stains of my life transformed me into the woman I am today.

We are conditioned to run from pain. It is the way we have survived, but it isn't the way we heal. When we're hurt, our deepest wounds are triggered. In response, we might run away, allowing our bodies to become numb under it, become small, turn on ourselves or lash out in anger. We sometimes feel our unforgiveness hurts the people who we feel are not worthy of forgiveness, but in essence, we inflict that hurt onto ourselves. Unforgiveness is a biting word from the ego, intended to project our pain onto the person who caused it. These words are often spoken in a desperate attempt to reject our circumstances. They express anger but are birthed from pain. Remember, hurt people hurt people.

Most people don't intentionally hurt others. Those who do are deeply pained themselves. Continuing to come back to this truth helped me to see my perpetrator's humanity, but even with that, there is still a tendency to demonize them. During the course of my life, I have tried mightily to understand what would make the perpetrators in my life make the choices they have made, and even when I couldn't understand it, I am still a work in progress trying to learn how to trust again.

The pain cut deeper than I realized and has affected other relationships, both positively and negatively. Positively, in that I continue to learn what I will not accept, the non-negotiables. We all have them. And negatively, in that I recall what I accepted in the past and the guilty cycle begins again in earnest. Forgiveness does not mean reconciliation. Sometimes the pain feels so deep that we can't imagine how we can ever forgive. Healing is a process. I would make progress, and when I thought I had forgiven, I'd suddenly find myself in a place of pain again.

We wrestle with trying to understand how someone could hurt us, especially those closest to us. How could you do this to me? These are words that fall out of the mouth in disbelief, the outcome of the heart and mind clashing together, wanting to understand. They are also spoken in an attempt to reject reality; the victim holds onto the past. For most of us, forgiveness isn't easy; I don't think it was meant to be. If forgiveness was easy, it may very well be a sign that we are repressing our pain. In contrast, when we're unable to forgive after long periods of time, resentment shows up.

We become self-oppressors because resentment says that you are wrong and bad, and I am good and victimized. It says that holding onto anger is the only way to heal, when, in fact, it is one of the things that keeps healing a stone's throw away, just beyond our grasp. Resentment claims a certain power over us while we pretend to have power over it. Resentment always wins. I resented until I realized I didn't have to fight it; I simply needed to turn my back to it.

I was angry at being angry until I found it to be a healthy place synonymous with crying. It became cleansing, as long as I didn't rest there for too long. I allowed the anger to do its job, and then I let it go. Forgiveness doesn't mean there is the absence of anger. That is a lesson I've learned the hard way.

I have loved and lost in love; people have broken my heart. Some of them were lovers and others were friends. In most cases, I used anger to protect my heart. I turned them into a villain, cut them out, and kept it moving. Then one day someone broke my heart, and it was different.

I never knew that someone could be her. I would never have believed that my mother would cut me so deeply. Her betrayal was worse than the molestation. I didn't love my stepfather and couldn't care less if he stayed or left. But she was different. My soul stepped in and said, "Nope. We're not doing it that way anymore. We are never going to love or trust like that. It is overrated. It's time to face the truth." So, I did, and I learned how much it can hurt to heal and how much more it can hurt not to.

We walk around traversing this world hurting each other. We lose control and sight of why we are here. People no longer look like people with beating hearts. We have become indispensable to each other. Sometimes we can't deal with our own pain, so we act unconsciously and, in turn, hurt those we care about. Other times, we choose to let someone go because their presence in our lives no longer serves us. Truth be told, I have been there. I have had to release people throughout my life because we were moving down different paths. I have had to remove toxic people, even family from my life because it hurt too much to keep them there as placeholders watching and waiting to see me fail at something or everything.

I do not believe that blood makes us family. I believe inextricably bound love and affinity for each other makes a family. There are people in my life who do not have the same blood as I, who have championed me through life—both good and bad times—and love me through it without batting an eye. Although the way we handle these situations makes a huge difference in the healing process, they both produce pain.

I have often questioned why victims are looked upon with disdain and questioning eyes, and yet, the perpetrators are given the benefit of the doubt, a pass or a slap on the wrist. Victims must prove that what happened to them is actually true, except I would not allow myself to carry that unnecessary burden. My truth was not and is not about proving it to be so; it is about shining a light on it so that I could illuminate my dark places and heal because light does not only reflect the beautiful places.

It is my hope that you, yes you, will lift a word or two from the pages of this book to help you remember why you are here, to remind you, too, that you are uniquely your own and you are good enough. No matter the stain, no matter the hurt or disappointments, you are one step away from living your best life, embracing the rain that washes away the stains and allows you to flourish. You deserve more than the defeat. Square your shoulders and rise up. God bless.

"Don't feel guilty for doing what is right for you, for in doing so, you live in divine providence."

~ Lynn Hall

FOREWORD

This is not your traditional foreword, but then again, this book is far from traditional. My name is Ra'Mon (or "baby boy"as my mom calls me); aka "brother" (as my sister calls me). I am her first born, and I have seen this woman struggle through so much adversity, only to always make sure that I was good growing up when it was just the two of us. Words can't explain the emotion I feel as I am writing this. My sister and I have the pleasure of introducing you to our mother as an author, as she shares her life's journey and experiences with you. This moment is mine to share my appreciation for my wonderful mother.

When I was young, I was surrounded by a huge family in Vero Beach, Florida. Aunts, uncles, cousins, you name it, and I would see some of them every week at my grandma's house while my mom was working multiple jobs. My Uncle Ken or Uncle Tom watched over me and my cousins. I always had somewhere to go. But then my mom and I moved away, and it literally became just us, a single black mother raising a young man.

I remember walking to the grocery store on the highway, just the two of us during Christmas, when she would buy me what she could afford. McDonald's used to be a treat for me. She did this with a smile, all just to make me believe everything was okay. I never had a relationship with my biological father and still don't to this day, but when I tell you that my mom played the role of mother and father to a "T," I mean it. I have never longed for that relationship because she was always there.

As a kid, I really thought this was how it was supposed to be, just the two of us, my mom and me, so I was always happy. Even in the few relationships she had over the years, I only cared about her well-being, until my little sister came along. Then, two became three, just the three of us. Enter Davida...

My name is Davida McCovery, the little sister to Ra'Mon and "baby girl" to your author, Lynn Hall. I'm so proud of my mom for achieving this goal. I love that despite all the obstacles she has faced, she has never forgotten her hopes and dreams. I have a father, but unfortunately, he has not been very present in my life, especially not in the way that my mother was and is to me and for me. As a single, African-American mother of a young daughter, she comforted me in our happy and sad days.

I remember we used to have our weekend getaways where we'd go shopping and eat lunch at parks nearby. I remember us always making memories no matter what our situation was. Having a father who was emotionally and mentally abusive to my mother, I always remember wanting to protect her. She is so precious to me, and I always wanted to shield her from suffering. I admire my mom, and I love her so dearly. I love having her as a role model, protector, mentor, mother and my best friend. Although our family may be small, it has a bond like no other.

Sure, it would be pleasing to say that our family, beyond the three of us, has always been close, but this would not be accurate. In the midst of the hardships, our mother has always been the glue that bonded us together.

As time has elapsed, my brother and I have learned the struggles that our mom has gone through since she was a young girl. She lost her father when she was very young, and that forced her to face the lack of trust and hurt from troubled relationships with family members, people that should have loved and cared the most about her.

This masterpiece, *Guilty Stains*, paints the picture of my mom's life from childhood through much of the present. We, as her children, and you as readers, will be taken on an emotional, yet powerful journey that captures her spiritual awakening and newfound self-love. My mom has shared her life with us both in some detail and hesitantly at times, but there are still things about her life we may not know. True to form, she asked my brother and I to read the book with her before sharing it with the world. We chose not to do that because this book is *her* story, not ours. This book will introduce us to more of her early life and things she has shielded us from. We are nervous and anxious, but most of all, we are happy to have this book in our hands; we know you will be too.

There is so much to say about this wonderful woman of God. She selflessly possesses the roles of mother, caretaker, nurturer, leader, motivator, friend, entrepreneur, free-thinker and so many other amazing gifts. We have always pushed each other to accomplish great things in life, and along the way, we have never forgotten one another. Our mother is the complete embodiment of success. She was the first to show us how to accomplish great things in life.

Lynn Hall has the spiritual gift of encouraging others and bringing faith to those around her. First, her tree of faith began within herself, and she held fast to this faith, which has led her to success.

We now introduce to you a beautiful body of work, your light in the dark places... *Guilty Stains.*

GS 1

The Stain of Molestation

*"People who abuse and molest generally
hunt where they are trusted."*
~ Tami Kab

She was quiet. She was reverent, always observant. She could be a trickster with her younger siblings and even with other younger kids from the neighborhood, but only if she knew you well. She lived in the land of make-believe, a fantasy world she created early in her young life as a safe haven. In that land of make-believe, she created a character named "Bloody Mary." Bloody Mary was an awesome looking woman with blood dripping from her toothless mouth. Serpents adorned her head, and her hands harbored 10-foot long nails that would claw out the eyes of anyone who was unkind to her or who misbehaved. All she had to do was call upon Bloody Mary by chanting her name three times, and she would appear to save the little girl.

The kids believed it, and whenever the young girl was asked to babysit, this mantra kept them in line. She'd begin the chant of "Bloody Mary," and the kids would scurry off screaming, "No, no, no, help us! Bloody Mary is coming!" She'd belly laugh about this for an hour or more. It would be the only real laughter she could fully own and fully experience for most of her childhood. The figment of "Bloody Mary" was a secret, and she would learn to keep many secrets over her lifetime.

She is me, a little girl with wide-eyed wonder, a sweet, innocent smile and sad eyes. I liken my stature to that of a banana. A banana ripens over time and goes from pale yellow, green in places to a very dark yellowish brown in a matter of days. It changes from being very hard and firm to soft and mushy and very sweet on the inside. Because of the stain of molestation at a very young age by my stepfather, my countenance was much different. I morphed from sweet and innocent to hard, resilient and defiant.

Strangely enough, even though the molestation muted me in so many ways, I actually found my voice in other ways. I began to speak my mind without choosing my words carefully. That became a part of the defiance because if nobody cared that this man was molesting me night in and night out, why should I care that the words I chose to wield would hurt the person on the receiving end. No, when the world started to care about me, maybe I'd start to care about it. I became very angry and learned early on that hurt people truly do hurt people.

My father died in a car accident when I was just three years old. My mother remarried several years later, and the man she would choose to marry was a vile human being. He is the reason I began to resent the sun going down. I thought the sunset was beautiful when I wasn't at home to endure the abuse as night fell. It was so magical, and I was in awe of the beautiful colors in the sky. All those colors condensed into one—red—when I was at home as the night took away the color of sunshine. Interestingly enough, red is now my favorite color because it represents the pain, the guilt and the stains of my life, but it also represents triumph, resilience and love.

My stepfather would come into my room, as I slept, touch me on the leg, and beckon me from my bed to him. He'd usher me into the family room with all the lights still off, sit me on the couch, spread my legs and perform oral sex on me. He'd stick his fingers inside my secret place and thrust them back and forth. He would decide how many fingers, and the more fingers he used, the more "gifts" he'd give me the next day. He'd hide them in one of my drawers and tell me I would continue to get them if I was a good girl and that good girls didn't tell secrets. He'd ask, "You are daddy's good little girl, aren't you?" He'd leave me candy and other knick-knacks that I loved, but I would have to hide to eat them. If I didn't, everyone would want to know where I got them, and he didn't want me to be forced to answer those questions because he was "protecting me," so he would say, over and over again. He is the reason my view of being protected became so skewed.

Our family room was in the back of the house, and there was a long window toward the back of the room. Off that room was a screened patio. When my oldest brother would leave to go out at night, he'd leave the door to the patio unlocked so he could sneak in through the family room without anyone knowing what time he came in.

One particular night, my stepfather had just pulled me from my bed and sat me at the edge of the couch. I was crying. This night, I was extremely angry and told him I didn't care about the gifts; I wanted it to stop. He told me he would tell my mom that I had misbehaved and get me into trouble if I didn't let him do it. I began to cry harder as I smelled his breath and the scent of him as he stuck one, then two fingers into my secret place, and turned them from left to right. I couldn't take it anymore. I pushed him from me and went to the bathroom, crying and washing myself and wondering why, oh why, was this happening to me. Please, anyone, make it stop.

Late the next afternoon, most of my siblings and I (there were a total of eight of us) were in the garage which housed a pool table. My oldest brother loved playing pool, and I loved doing anything he loved unbeknownst to him. He's the reason I love professional football and basketball. It was my excuse to sit in silence with him whenever he watched television. He didn't say much, but he was just present, and I felt safe when he was around. I loved him more than he probably knew because he represented strength and the presence of my father, who was no longer there. Even though I didn't know my father well, my brother was a pretty good representation of what I imagined he was like.

My mother came into the garage and began to chastise my brother for coming in too late again. My brother was clearly angry and rebellious, especially after what he had just witnessed the night before. At the time, I had no idea he had witnessed the abuse firsthand. As my mother continued to chastise him, he finally lashed out and said that she had the nerve to get on him when she married a monster who he had witnessed messing with his little sister and then pointed to me. Sitting on top of the washer with one of my sisters, I was mortified and didn't know how to respond. All eyes turned to me and there was momentary silence. I dropped my head.

My mother called him a liar and told him to get out of her house. My brother, my protector, my football-watching buddy, packed his things and left our home, the home my father built before his death, and never returned. It was what my stepfather wanted all along, and I was devastated.

How could my mother never even ask me if it was true or not? How could she ignore the truth? I've carried the guilty stain of molestation around for a long time, believing that it was my fault and I somehow caused it due to the fact my mother muted me. She either did or didn't believe my brother but was too afraid to face the consequences of that reality, and as a result, chose to ignore the inner voice that may have held her truth and mine. Either way, I suffered because of her ignorance in looking the other way.

Never before did I feel so small, and for a time, I would welcome this feeling because it wrapped me into an embrace; not that of a loving one, but of a familiar comfort because knowing felt better than uncertainty. While foreign initially, yet somewhat familiar because of the molestation I endured, I hesitated to welcome it because I knew it was not my truth.

Despite how I felt as a 7-year-old child when this man was introduced into my life, I continued to be abused and muted through middle school where I reclaimed my voice. I remember exactly when it occurred. I had asked my mother if I could attend a middle school basketball game after school. One of the basketball players was my next-door neighbor, and I was quite smitten with him. My mother initially said I could not attend. Surprisingly enough, she was quite strict with us and would not allow us to wear pants, jewelry, make-up, etc. until middle and high school.

We were finally allowed to start wearing some of these things through bribery by my stepfather. He would force me to allow him to do certain things to me so that my sisters and I could be like other girls our age. After I gave in, he would then convince our mother to allow us to do whatever was "on the table" when he performed indecent acts on me. For instance, he would perform oral sex on me and stick his fingers inside me in order to convince our mother to allow us to wear pants. When she agreed, he would come back to let me know. Later, my mother would announce it to us all. My sisters were elated when we were allowed to wear pants to school, but they had no idea what I had to endure to allow us that opportunity or benefit.

Such was the same instance when I asked to go to the game, except this time I said "no" to his advances. This time, I said I didn't care what he told my mother, but he would not touch me inappropriately again, or I would tell anyone who would listen. He had already agreed it was okay for me to go after another of his sex acts and even bought me a jersey in my school colors for me to wear to the game.

My friend, who was the sister of the player I liked, and I were in the stands as the game was beginning that evening. All of a sudden, I heard my name over the loudspeaker summoning me to the office. As I approached the lady at the desk, she asked if I was Calenthia, and I said, "yes." She handed me the phone and said my mother was on the line. When I got on the phone, my mother was livid. She informed me that my stepfather told her I had snuck off after school with the next-door neighbor. I swore to her it wasn't true and that my stepfather told me I could go to the game. I informed her he was fully aware. She chose not to believe me, even though I was the child she always touted who could be relied on for anything, including taking care of my younger siblings. Yet, in this instance, she again chose to believe someone other than me. I, again, felt like a mute, and again, my mother was on the other end, not to empower, but to silence.

She informed me she was on her way to the school to pick me up, and I had better be waiting in front of the school. I was there and so was she moments later. I showed her the jersey he had secretly bought for me and asked her how could he not know when he bought the jersey. She said she didn't believe he bought it and that my stepfather told her my next-door neighbor bought it. I was petrified. We sat in terrifying silence the short drive home where I was whipped and punished for "sneaking off with my boyfriend." True to form, my stepfather told his lies, and she believed him over me.

That day forever changed the way I saw my mother. I began to see her as weak, naïve and blind to what was happening right before her. Her daughter was being molested—internally and externally—and with pleading eyes and a longing heart, wanting her mom to somehow save her from it, protect her from it. That never happened ; I had to take control of my own life at all costs. I didn't learn until much later in life that my stepfather reached out to my next-door neighbor and threatened him to stay away from me and forbade him to ever speak to me again. You see, he wanted me all to himself, and the fact that a boy was interested in me was not acceptable.

I wondered why the boy never spoke to me again and would ignore me in the halls at school. I was so devastated because I thought I was in love. I was in love with the way he treated me. He made me laugh. He helped me to forget the stains I felt everyone around me could see. He made me feel invisible, in a good way, because if people didn't see me, they couldn't see the stains. I just wanted him to see me, but he stopped. His absence from my life caused me to feel dirty again, so dirty, nobody wanted to keep me around for very long, including him.

I remember when one of my older sisters moved out of our home. She sensed our stepfather was sexually abusing my younger sister and me because he had also made advances on her, but she was much more strong-willed than I was at the time, though times have changed.

She would ask me and my younger sister several times if he was doing things to me. She even had a conversation with our grandmother, my mother's mother, to let her know what was happening. My oldest brother had conversations with the very same grandmother, and they chastised him for saying anything. I suppose the generational curses of molestation, incest and abuse was so familiar to them, they did not see any of it as a problem. So, my brother, too, was silenced into submission. Even though there were questions, nobody bothered to extract me from the situation.

Didn't they know that where there was smoke, inevitably there was fire? My stepfather had already told me I would have nowhere to live because I would suffer the same fate as my oldest brother if I uttered one word about what he was doing. So, of course, I kept his dirty little secrets and didn't tell a soul about what he was doing to me, not even my sister. It wasn't as if they would believe me anyway or at least, that is how I felt.

There came a time when I realized that my mother would not be my savior. I often wonder if she knew about the abuse but felt powerless underneath the weight of that notion. My mother was uneducated and found herself a widow at a very young age when my father died. When she met and married my stepfather, was this her way of not being alone, of not having to walk the road of life all alone, without my father or a man there to hold her up? Was she resentful of me because her perverted husband chose to molest a very young girl who happened to be her daughter? How could the one person who was supposed to protect me be the very one to hurt me worse than anyone else ever could? These are all questions I have asked myself over the years.

Sadly, I still do not know the answers to these questions. This is the elephant in the room that has remained there all my life. I've gotten comfortable with the elephant, as long as he didn't expect me to feed it. Now, I realized I could stare it down; I could see him and ignore him at the same time because the choice belonged to me. The choice I didn't own was whether or not my family wanted to see him and cast him out the room, so we could bridge the divide of our collective pains and stains and wash together.

Because of the molestation perpetrated by my stepfather, my youngest sister and I, especially, had a somewhat strained relationship. My youngest brother and I fared much better. I used to take him to work with me at the answering service. He and my son were like best friends. He protected my little guy, and I loved him so much for that.

The sexual perpetrator is not my father, though he is theirs. His blood does not course through my veins. Why didn't he molest his own daughter? She was in the home too. Why didn't he molest his own son? He was in the home too. Did I want that to happen? Of course not, but these are questions I posed to myself frequently in my younger years.

He purposefully chose to degrade and victimize me over and over again. I understand the emotions that my younger siblings must contend with on a regular basis. In many ways, I viewed my younger sister and me as the victims. I cannot imagine the plight she suffers when asked the name of her father. I could understand not wanting to share that for fear of taunts and reprisal. I am their sister, yet he is their father. It must be a difficult position, and I understand it. I expect them to love their father without condition. I expect for them to stand with him. Just as I expect for them to love their father, I also expect them to understand their father is not the man to me he is to them. He doesn't represent to and for me what he does to and for them.

You can imagine that as we got older and I would return home to visit, things would be a little awkward because my youngest sister wanted to invite her father to family functions when I was present. That was never going to happen because he is not my family, nor will he ever be so. This man did his best to break me in so many ways just to satisfy his own horrendous, skewed, disgusting sexual appetite for little girls. I saw in him a demonic monster and still do. He believes he can just move past being a pedophile with no intervention, but this is not true. Just as an alcoholic needs to seek help from that addiction, my stepfather needs help from his addiction. The problem with keeping this kind of secret means sharing in the addiction and being an enabler. It makes the perpetrator feel that what he did or has done is not so bad. The secrets have become a blanket that has shielded him from the truth for many years. Though his mind may never allow him to forget what he has done, his mind will never provide the same satisfaction or release. He will never be able to hide from it until he faces it. God offers forgiveness but not without acknowledgement and repentance.

There was a resolve within me that molestation could not diminish, no matter how painful and regardless of the fact that my past, my childhood held so many unanswered questions. Even though I was molested, I was not what he did to me. I could still choose who I was to become. His power could only go as far as I allowed it. He prided himself on keeping secrets because the secrets were a critical weapon both to entice and ensnare me into his sick world.

For children, keeping secrets gives a sense of importance, prestige and control. He wanted me to believe I was the only one in the world who would look out for him because if anyone knew of his evil and sinister deeds, he would be punished, and it would be all my fault. Keeping these secrets built up in him a feeling of equal responsibility and equal guilt in me, a totally innocent child. And it was this fear to inform on him without having to explain my own inability to stop him that kept me captive to his grotesque mind and hands.

When I was 13, I gave my life to Christ at Wabasso Church of God in Christ. One of my stepfather's aunts told me at that time that she believed I would be a "little light" unto the world. She said she could see it all over me when I gave my life to Christ. Even in those excruciating moments when I felt so small, I have never forgotten that. It was that light that helped me to climb out of the darkness. I looked for it every morning and found it in the smallest things, like music, an outfit, or fantasizing about a different life, one where everybody wanted to know me, and everyone thought I was more special than the next. I did not escape it unscathed because there are still times when the worst of it resurfaces as low self-esteem, lack of trust, anger, resentment, isolation and many other ways.

Sexual abuse is damaging no matter how the victim's body is violated. It doesn't matter if there is sexual intercourse or physical touching or kissing. It is still a violation and the violation continues when those closest to you doubt the veracity of your claim. The degree of trauma associated with my abuse included my relationship with my stepfather and his role in our family and the duration of the abuse. He snatched away my dignity and the beauty of my soul, the person I was becoming. The damage was akin to being struck by a Mack truck traveling 50 mph, and when you look back at yourself, you are unrecognizable.

The damage was in direct proportion to the degree that it disrupted the protection and nurturance of the parental bond. There were two issues related to the potential disruption ; the abuse and the revelation of the abuse. When the abuse was perpetrated, it set into motion the tremors of an internal earthquake that required a strong and nurturant environment to quell. I didn't experience or live in that type of environment. Because that environment was not available, I set aside the internal process of healing to ensure my own survival. A father is called to be a secure, trustworthy, and life-generating surrogate for God until the child develops the capacity to see his or her heavenly Father as the only perfectly trustworthy source of life. My struggle to trust was proportionately related to the extent my mother and stepfather failed to protect and nurture me as a child.

For a long time, I wanted to understand why he did it. Did I bring it on myself somehow? I rationalized that if I could just peek into his mind, maybe this understanding would prove it wasn't my fault. Why did he act out his sexual fantasies on me? I wanted to understand and shed light on the conditions and circumstances that caused him to want to be sexual with a child, even though he had a wife.

Before entering this battle ahead, I had to acknowledge that a battle existed. Facing the reality of my past abuse was a process. It did not happen quickly or in one climactic moment of honesty. It occurred over a lengthy time, during which the past abuse was seen in light of current choices of flight or fight. The memories of the past abuse were often accompanied with little emotion other than disbelief or incredulity. My memories of those events with my stepfather were separated from emotion, as if they were frozen in ice, seen and felt but not able to be touched. At other times, I would recall the memories in small details that seemed to have lost context, specificity or meaning. To open one's heart to a truth that is deeply devastating seems, at first, foolish; however, the hard, cold parts of our soul are continually tempted to thaw by the warmth of the longings of our soul. Every pleasant interchange is an invitation to life; every deep sorrow stirs the passion of grief. Those daily temptations to life are viewed by the person who has been sexually abused, at best, as a two-day vacation to a warm climate and, at worst, as the melting of the polar ice cap. A total meltdown spells disaster; therefore, the icy soul must remain frozen and hidden.

Many times, I tried, in my own mind, to deny the abuse, mislabel it, or at least minimize the damage. The enemy goes unrecognized or misunderstood, so I cannot fight the battle. Once the war is avoided, then something must be done with the wounded heart that cries out for solace and hope. The cry must be heard or squelched. Sadly, the choice is usually to stifle the groan. What normally mutes the cry is the internal dynamic that promotes denial, mislabeling or minimization. I felt I just didn't have the resources to win. The dynamic involved the subtle workings of guilt and contempt that served to keep my soul frozen and the warmth of life at a distance. I needed to be rescued from this dark place. God, the eraser of my stain of molestation, said unto me in Isaiah 1:18:

"Come now, and let us reason together, saith the Lord: though your sins be as scarlet, they shall be as white as now; though they be red like crimson, they shall be as wool."

The colors red and crimson had such a strong and pervasive psychological effect on me because it was reminiscent of blood, which was symbolic of the guilt I felt. Even though I was a young girl, I still felt the guilt of being touched by this monster over and over again. My supposed sin and guilt were grievous, obvious and permanent. I felt angry and forsaken by God. However, in the Scripture, Isaiah said sins and guilt can be made white as snow, as wool. White represents purity. So, when Isaiah says that the Lord can change our sins and guilt from scarlet or crimson to snow or wool, I knew he was professing the Lord can do something that is impossible for us to do on our own. A cloth dyed red stays red; it is permanent, but regardless of the stain, the Atonement of Jesus Christ would make me pure again. When I petitioned God about the guilt I felt, He reminded me I had been made whole and my perpetrator would be held accountable for the sins he committed against one of His lambs because the word says to bring the lambs unto Him. Rather than do that, my stepfather abused me mightily. Because God released me from the stain, I had to walk in it by doing several things.

Removal of the Stain of Molestation

1. **Building Trust** – I reminded myself repeatedly that I can be trusted, even when others cannot. I can now protect the little girl and talk to her and show her that we are okay. We made it from victim to victor and the stain helped to create a beautiful masterpiece, a work of art. The violation became a permanent part of my tapestry. The little girl in me suffered, but the adult in me gets the amazing job of protecting her now. In our pain, we have learned how to treat others who are wounded like us and advocate for them. That is why telling our story was so important. In order to help others like me, I had to unlock the arms of those who wanted to keep secrets and protect the perpetrators so that I could free my arms to lock with those who needed me most. I realized for my one story, there must be a million others who wanted so desperately to speak. This body of work is now their permission slip, their platform.

2. **Being Angry** – I learned it was okay to be angry about what happened to me. I wasn't crazy for feeling this great emotion. I also learned that while it was okay to feel this emotion, it had to be temporary; I couldn't live in this state. This feeling became a very healthy response to the pain. There were times I used other things to dull the pain but recognizing those patterns

helped me to rely on healing and moving forward, rather than binding myself to it.

3. **Grieving** – I grieved for the little girl in me for a very long time, and at times, when I am wounded again, I still do. I run to her because she is so very beautiful with sad eyes that still remind me of hope. I am hopeful for every little girl who has encountered the same fate. I often wonder who the little girl may have been if the molestation had never touched her. I grieved for a lost childhood. I grieved because I couldn't help her when she needed me most. I just grieved. I learned it was okay because she is me, and we are okay.

4. **Moving forward** – I am a victor, not just a survivor, no longer a victim. I acknowledged my past and the pain of it but did not allow it to define me. I believed with everything in me that I was strong enough to move forward. I am who I am today because of my past.

I didn't choose my mom or stepfather. I was born to my mom and given away by her to my stepfather. I am sure she didn't think she was turning me over to a vile human being who would take no thought for violating me in the worst way. I don't believe that was her intent.

Because I don't feel loved by my mother does not mean that she doesn't love me in her own way. I would be a different Lynn, not better, not worse, just different, had I been given another mother and father. I know my life would have been much different had my father not been tragically killed in that awful accident.

What I know for sure is that because I experienced what I did, I understand the heart of another in the way only those who share a history of childhood abuse can understand. Of this, I am certain: if I can do it, so can you. I believed I had made it through the worst of it and was able to see over the mountain that had towered over me for most of my life... until the next stain was introduced into my life... the Stain of Single Motherhood.

*"If I were to remain silent,
I'd be guilty of complicity."*

~ Albert Einstein

GS 2

The Stain of Single Motherhood

"There will be so many times you feel like you've failed, but in the eyes, heart and mind of your child, you are Super Mom."
~Stephanie Precourt

I was to be the first child to graduate from high school and go to college. I was well on my way and had begun searching for colleges. I didn't have many friends in school, so most of the people I associated with were cousins. I watched as other girls my age were so well-liked, so pretty, so popular, and I longed to be like many of them. It was well-known that the "Hall girls" led strict lives by a mother who believed girls should be seen and not heard. We were either at church or at school; there wasn't a whole lot we could do in between. Living in a Pentecostal Christian household meant we couldn't wear pants, no nail polish, no secular music, no parties, no boyfriends, etc.

The older I got, the more I reflected on how hypocritical I believed my mother to be. All this... going to church on Sundays and on Wednesdays for Bible Study, Vacation Bible School, singing in the choir, etc. On the surface, we looked like the Brady Bunch, but when you delve just a little deeper, you barely scratch the surface of our lives. We were always conditioned to keep family business at home. That ate me alive, and for many years, I told my kids the same thing. I no longer tell them that because whatever they need to share to feel better about themselves or to unplug the plug that has caused them to labor in their breathing is not acceptable to me. I want always to be a part of their healing and growth, never their pain.

Before I became a single mother, I used to pride myself on not being a statistic, despite being raised by a single mother for some time before my mother remarried. I just knew I would have the fairy tale life complete with the white picket fence. I still wanted to experience the fairy tale. I wanted to experience the big and little moments and milestones that I believed were meant to be shared by two parents, not one young girl still living at home with all hopes of going to college a distant memory. Unfortunately, I was alone, and single motherhood took on a whole new life of its own; two lives at that.

But 31 years ago, I faced that fate. It became apparent very early on that the relationship I was in that had created life was, in fact, dead. Our relationship wasn't one based on or filled with love, but it had somehow managed to create it. And because of that, I chose life, the life of my unborn child.

Enduring pregnancy is tough enough all by itself, but coupled with being a teenaged mom-to-be increased the difficulty times one thousand. I really liked my child's father, and I often imagined him wanting so much to be in our lives, raising our child together, but that was not to be. He was a womanizer who impregnated two young girls at the same time. If memory serves, she had her child just a couple of months prior to me having mine. For some strange reason, she was fixated on my child and me, showing up at the hospital to take a peek at my child as if he were an animal at the local zoo. I found it very odd, but as it turns out, she was very territorial over this man despite all the things he did to her, and the world he promised her had also been promised to other women, including me.

I knew a lot would be said about me as a single mother because my sisters and I faced jealousy from other girls all the time. We lived well, thanks to my father. I expected the slander and vitriol about who I had become as a young woman, my decision-making, and the very nature of my sexual being was up for judgement and ridicule. I just wanted to run and hide. How could I allow this to happen? I was young, beautiful and smart and was well on my way to a paid scholarship to college.

Nothing could be said about me that I didn't think about myself. I didn't even want to consider dating because I knew how difficult that would be as a single mother. I considered myself damaged goods and unworthy of the type of love that I wanted, that I craved. It seemed it would never come true for me; I would never see my fantasy play out in real life. The love I imagined was elusive for sure now, and I had myself to blame. My body, which I wasn't really in love with prior to pregnancy, was now a fixer-upper in need of desperate repairs. I didn't like my big belly and skinny legs. I looked like an oversized flamingo. I began to hate the person I saw staring back at me in the mirror. There was a reason nobody stayed in her life. She just wasn't suited for the long haul.

No matter how I felt before my son was born, seeing him eliminated it all. I would pretend not to be happy when others were around because I imagined what they would think of me. How could I be happy about being a single mother? It was so easy. That little boy needed me, and I desperately needed him. God gave us to each other because He knew best the love I craved, and He knew even better who could provide that kind of agape, earthly love. My son did that for me the day he was born and still does today. Oh, how I love that young man. He gave me so much.

Sure, I was afraid of raising a young man. The questions were many: How can I, as a woman, raise a boy to be a man? How could I answer the inevitable questions he would surely have as a boy entering school? What would I tell him about the birds and the bees? I knew those kinds of questions were coming, but the funny thing is, my son made answering all those questions easy because he never asked. We still had the conversations, but he was the most thoughtful, most forgiving and understanding child I could not have imagined him to be. He made my life easier, not harder.

I found that I focused on my true feelings about being a single parent very often. Not because I didn't like it, but because I felt the weight of my guilt. Guilt that I was not able to give him what other kids would receive at birthdays and Christmas. I felt the guilt of him not experiencing what it must have been like to have a father in his life. My son and I grew up to know what that feeling was like together. I learned that when I focused on my true feelings, it was like reopening a wound, except the pain of reopening it allowed it to heal that much faster. My son was like the ointment or antibiotic that healed that wound right up. He just has that way about him.

Much to popular and contrary belief, it never occurred to me to be angry and bitter. I was sadder and more disappointed during this time of my life. I just wanted more for my son because I believed he deserved it. I felt like he got the short end of the stick. I don't think of the contributor any more than I'm sure he thinks of me. I make more space for guilt, shame, and regret instead.

That trio is heavier than a sleeping child to carry. They cannot be shed entirely—only packed away under the responsibilities of daily life, and at the top of that list was that of keeping another human being alive. Every so often, the trio rears their ugly heads, and I welcome them as another dragon to slay.

My longing to be liked, coupled with the abuse of my childhood, caused me to be very irrational and to make emotional decisions. There was a very popular guy in high school that I liked a lot. He was a star on the football team, dressed really cool and had lots of friends, male and female. I didn't think he ever noticed me, so when he approached me in the hallway after class one day, I was surprised and elated. He read me very well because he took advantage of my affinity for him. Day after day, he would say a little more and a little more.

Then, finally one day, he suggested I leave campus with him for lunch. I was mortified because I had never skipped school and never even thought of leaving campus without permission. Yet, on this day, I did it. I left campus with him without even hesitating because I knew if I didn't, he would probably never speak to me again and would view me as a nerdy girl. This act of leaving campus with him made me feel like I fit in with the cool kids; I had secured my spot within the "in" crowd by virtue of this great looking, popular guy. I may have been book-smart, but street sense eluded me like a loose woman avoiding church.

We went to his house and within minutes, we were upstairs in his bedroom having sex, unprotected sex. I was so scared. After the act, he took me back to campus and nobody ever found out I had left. The guy acted as if he didn't even know me. I quickly realized I was just another score for him, as if he was scoring a touchdown on the football field. If my self-esteem was low before I consummated this sexual act with him, it was almost non-existent afterwards.

A couple of months later, I realized "that time of the month" wasn't coming. My mom started asking questions. I even resorted to putting ketchup in my panties and tossing them into the dirty clothes hamper, so my mom wouldn't suspect anything. One night as I prepped for my bath, I had just got into the bathtub when my mom knocked on the door and asked to come in. I knew I was doomed because I had nowhere to hide. My stomach had started to grow and there was no hiding it in the bathtub.

She walked in and sat down on the toilet. She stared at my stomach and asked me if I was pregnant. I told her, "no" because I had just had my period. I showed her my panties with the ketchup stain, and she started to shake her head back and forth. She said, "You are pregnant. Who have you had sex with and when?" I couldn't hide it. I had to tell her what happened. So, I did. She didn't yell, she didn't berate me in that moment, and she didn't tell me how disappointed she was, though clearly that was evident.

The next day after school, we talked about it. She called my aunt who lived in Miami and explained it all to her. She told my stepfather, although I didn't like him knowing. Even though we lived under the same roof—which was a living hell—he and I barely spoke. After devising a plan for my mom and I to go to Miami to research doctors who would abort my child, I was told not to tell anyone else I was pregnant. Of course, yet again, I didn't have a voice or choice in the matter. So, I went along with the plan.

At the end of the week, we were on our way to Miami. After going to several doctors, doctor after doctor said I was too far along to abort the child. They each said my life would be at risk because the child was fully formed, as I was nearly four months pregnant. Hopes of keeping another secret were dashed. We drove back home, with my mom saying I could not go to college. I had to take care of my child. I was terrified.

We told my siblings, and I don't know how they felt. I felt I had let so many people down. I felt guilty because I had gone along with a plan to abort a life. Yet, God had other plans for me, for us. My son was born January 7, 1987.

His father never knew about the plan to abort. He wouldn't have cared either way, as he wanted no part of our child's life. The first and only willing contribution he gave to our child was a pack of 100 diapers that he brought to my mother's house and left at the edge of the driveway. Beyond that, he gave nothing. I decided at that point that I would never ask him for another thing as long as I lived. I now had another life for which I was responsible, and this would become the most important job of my entire life.

After graduating from high school, I got a job, an apartment and began the tough job of supporting my child and me. College, indeed, had to wait. My mother was a huge help with him, taking care of him while I was at work, buying him clothes and doing other things to help provide for him. I will forever be grateful to her for that.

My son and I weathered many storms together. He is so forgiving, so understanding, and he loves his mom without condition. God had a plan for his life and mine. He has helped me to grow in ways I cannot count. God knew I would need him desperately throughout my lifetime, and he would need me. We taught each other what love looks like. I taught him that even though relationships fail, I refused to turn my identity over to the failures. I refused to get mired down by the guilt I experienced by getting pregnant, attempting to abort and delaying college.

I suffered with so much guilt after my son was born. I wanted to provide a better life for him. He was not born with an instruction manual, so I had to create one. Part of doing that was to, again, create fantasy. When I couldn't afford meat, I would buy Spam and fry it up and act really excited about it because it was something new. I would say to him, "Look what I'm making for dinner. I found this great recipe I think you'll like." I didn't want him to know it was all I could afford.

The holidays were the worst because he would see all his friends with the great gifts, and yet I could only afford small things, like a football or board game. He never, ever complained, not once. I think he knew and chose to make life easier for me. I knew that I needed to be better for him, and part of that work included removing the stains of guilt.

In the end, I knew that all I could do was to be the best mom to my son as possible. I was not able to give him a father, but he promised me that I was absolutely the best father a son could have asked for. Maybe he says that because he doesn't know any better because if you've never had something or experienced it, how can you know what it feels like not to have it? Either way, my heart melts every Father's Day when he calls to wish me a wonderful day. That young man loves and adores his mom, and he is a big reason why I was able to erase the guilty stains of single motherhood. He saw me through eyes of wonder; he made me feel like 'super mom,' even when I didn't feel my best was good enough. God knew what He was doing and how He and my son would be the erasers I needed at this moment in my life.

God, the eraser of my stain of single motherhood, said unto me in Genesis 21:18-20:

18"Lift the boy up and take him by the hand, for I will make him into a great nation. 19Then God opened her eyes and she saw a well of water. So, she went and filled the skin with water and gave the boy a drink. [20]God was with the boy as he grew up."

This scripture reminded me that though Hagar engaged in sin with Abraham at the urging of Abraham's wife, Sarah, God was still with her son. I was encouraged to enter into a new life with my son by removing the guilty stains I felt as a single mother.

Removal of the Stain of Single Motherhood

1. **Practicing self-forgiveness** – I learned to forgive—my mom, my son's father and me. I had to take on the role of mother and father, and I wanted my son to know I could excel at both. I didn't want him to learn limitations from me, nor did I want to be the reason he learned the definition of the word, "crutch." To be healthy and whole, forgiveness was a must and I had to be the example to show him how to love, even when people weren't so lovable.

2. **Ignoring judgments** – People have their own idea of what life is like for single moms and why single moms are single. I quickly realized I could not own others' perception of me as a woman or mother because, really, it's none of my business. The more I focused on the judgments, the less aware I became at realizing how those judgments affected my son and me. I would become angry and bitter. No, I turned bitter into better.

3. **Practicing self-love** – I did not need validation from anyone because my life is my own. I had to realize I didn't need someone else to complete me. Sure, I wanted genuine love from another person, but when I embraced self-love, I finally understood another person only adds to that in a different way but who I am, as a single mother, was not diminished because

who or what the other person may add to my life. I began to pursue my dreams at all costs and fought through many storms with focus, determination and drive. I became more confident, stronger and self-assured in the process.

I struggled with whether to include the thought to abort my child because I did not want to include anything that would cause pain without a purpose for it. Then, I realized that not including it would cause me to actively participate in the secret. I discussed what transpired with my son because his heart, his feelings mattered to me greatly. My kids have supported me from beginning to end, and this time was no different. My son gave me his full support, understanding that his presence, his being here on this earth was for the Master's greater purpose. Though not planned, he was no accident, and it was important for him to understand that.

I also wanted him to know how much he is and always has been loved. When circumstances made the decision for us, my mother fully embraced my child and did all that she could to support him. I could not have accomplished all I did in those early days without her sharing the load of taking care of my child. She treated him as if she had birthed him, and for that, she has my enduring and undying love and respect.

In 1 Kings 19:5, Scripture says, *"Then he lay down and slept under the broom tree. But as he was sleeping, an angel touched him and told him, 'Get up and eat!'"* because Elijah's journey ahead would be a long one and he would need his strength. I am grateful for the experiences and growth I have had as a single mom. I would need every ounce of that strength to survive the storm that was brewing... the Stain of a Mother's Betrayal.

GS 3

The Stain of a Mother's Betrayal

"Family is supposed to be our safe haven. Very often, it's the place where we find the deepest heartache."
~ Iyanla Vanzant

For as long as I can remember, I wanted so much to be loved and wanted. These deep emotions caused me to become a people-pleaser. It is often said the middle child tends to be ignored or overlooked because of her place in the family. So, I took my place as a middle child but wanted desperately to be noticed. I believe it is this need that caused my stepfather to molest me—the quiet, reserved, shy little girl. My mother would always say that I was "just like her" because I kept the house clean and made sure the younger kids were cleaned and fed. The more she heaped these kinds of accolades onto me, the more I wanted to please her. So, all the things I did, I did to please her.

Even after my oldest brother left our home, I hoped my mother would ask me about the molestation. After days, weeks then months went by and the molestation continued, I knew that question would never come. I became even more withdrawn, sullen, and stayed to myself in my bedroom most of the time except for the occasional Saturdays when she would ask me to come with her and my grandmother to the laundromat and the grocery store. I loved to go with them because it gave me a chance to hear all the gossip and figure out who they were going to talk about. I liked listening to this adult conversation, but I couldn't engage because children were supposed to "stay in a child's place." Even still, being away from home took me away from the abuse I was suffering.

After I became pregnant and had my son, my mother was a great help. I didn't worry about whether my son was taken care of while I was at work because she'd pick him up from daycare when she got off work and take him home with her until it was time for me to get off. He loved spending this time with her, and I loved the idea they spent so much time together as well. Unfortunately, this is where my mother's "motherly instincts" began and ended.

I cannot recall a time when I felt nurtured or how often I was told "I love you" or received hugs for no apparent reason from my mother. At the time, I didn't realize how disconnected she was from her children emotionally. It wasn't until I became an adult and had children of my own that I realized I didn't know how to show this type affection because I didn't have an example. I learned how to show my children love by just doing it. That's what you do when there is a void; you fill it with good or you fill it with bad. It's a choice.

After having my son, I remained at my mother's home for a short time while working to take care of my child. My days consisted of taking my son to daycare, going to work, picking him up in the evenings, going home and preparing dinner and pressing repeat for the next day. My son was my life, so anything outside of taking care of him was very foreign to me.

One evening after leaving work, I went to the gas station. As I was filling my gas tank, a man approached me and asked if he could pump and pay for my gas. I was still very naïve and didn't quite know how to respond to his offer, but I reluctantly agreed to allow him to pay, not pump. After he paid, he came out of the store and gave me a card with his telephone number and asked if he could take me on a date. He was a police officer and was dressed in his uniform. There was a hospital close by, and he said he had 24-hour duty guarding a prisoner at the hospital. He asked if I could come by later to visit with him as he worked. This felt safe enough—weird, but safe—so I told him I would think about it.

That day, my mother picked my son up from daycare as she typically would, and I shared with her what had transpired. When I told her the man was white, she scoffed at that. She was not really open to me dating a white man. I found out later the man was Italian, but she still did not like that notion. I couldn't understand why she dismissed it or why she was so opposed to it. Initially, I thought she just didn't want me dating a man of another race, but that wasn't the case at all. Her feelings toward him would soon change in dramatic fashion, as she would assume the role of his mistress. No longer did she view him as a white man dating her daughter; she would come to know him intimately as the white man who would become her lover.

See, my mother and I were extremely close when I became a young adult. We were more like sisters than mother and daughter, and the rest of my siblings knew it. They called me "her favorite." We would go shopping together nearly every Saturday and get our hair and nails done. We'd have lunch, and I could talk to her about any and everything. She was a great listener as I got older, but something started to change in our relationship. It felt like secrets were beginning to unravel in our relationship. I could not have known just how much.

After talking with my mother that night and sharing the details of my conversation with the man I had met, even though she didn't think I should go, I went to the hospital to meet him anyway. I felt the environment was safe. When I got there, he met me at the elevator, just outside the prisoner's room. He said he was happy to see me again, and now that I knew he was a police officer and wasn't going to harm me, he wanted to take me out on an official date.

Before doing that, I wanted him to meet my mother. So, our first date was inviting him to her house. She was cold at first but started to relax and warm up to him. After he left, I asked her what she thought of him, and she said, "He's alright." Having my mother's half-approval of him, we started dating.

Things seemed to go very well initially until he started to display anger towards my son. One evening after picking my son up from daycare, I stopped for dinner—burgers and fries. My son liked to eat his food on the floor of the living room while watching television. For some unknown reason, this man became enraged, stomped on my son's food, and told him to "eat it now." Needless to say, my soon-to-be-husband never did that again.

We eventually got married and moved about 20 minutes away from my mother's house, however, it wasn't long before I wanted out. I suspected he had been cheating and shared this with my mother, as I did about everything. She dismissed it as me being too suspicious or too jealous because she didn't believe my husband would ever cheat on me because he loved me too much. As I mentioned before, I rarely deviated from my day-to-day routine, so much of the "noise" going on in the community about my husband's philandering ways came as a surprise to me. I was clueless but pretty much ignored what I thought were rumors. I would soon discover there was a whole lot of truth to those rumors.

I noticed that every time my mother would come around, he would act as though we were having issues in our marriage, and he wouldn't come close to me. Instead, he would sit close to my mother, and they would chat, and she'd giggle like a schoolgirl having her first crush. Every now and again, their attention would turn to me with a question or a comment, and then I'd become invisible again.

I began to have thoughts that my mother and husband were seeing each other. I would quickly dismiss those thoughts because what kind of mother would do that? My mother and I had a sister-like relationship, and I could not imagine she would do something like that. I beat myself up over and over again for having those thoughts. Those thoughts would never leave me.

So, I scheduled lunch with my mother, just the two of us. Halfway through our meal, I asked her how she would respond and if she would tell me if my husband were to show interest or flirt with her. Her response confirmed what I already knew to be true. She said very mildly, "Of course, I'd tell you." Knowing my mother, this was the complete opposite of what I would have expected. I expected incredulousness at my audacity to suggest she would even entertain such behavior, much less to question whether or not she'd share it with me. That is the type of response I was hoping to hear from the woman who gave birth to me, the woman who was supposed to protect me, not intentionally cause me harm. However, she laughed it off, and that hurt immeasurably.

I left lunch that day with so many conflicting emotions and questions? Was I wrong? Could I be wrong? This is my mother. Was she right? Would she tell me? What kind of person was I for even allowing this kind of thought to enter my mind? Was I going crazy? That last question would torment me for a long time until my questions, or at least this question, was answered.

During the course of my marriage and my thoughts of an ensuing relationship between my mother and my husband, the two of them would routinely advise me to press charges against my stepfather. They would do this separately, so as not to appear to be a team working together to remove him from the picture. I would learn later that my stepfather had known for a long time that my husband and mother were having an affair. They threatened that if he uttered a word to me, they would have him arrested as being a pedophile. My stepfather did not know the wheels were already in motion. They worked me like a potter with clay. It was perfection because I was so naïve, I did not realize what was happening.

Finally, I was convinced. My husband was a police officer and asked his counterparts at work what I needed to do to press charges against my stepfather. Because the statue of limitations had run out, I was told by a detective that I would have to meet with him and get him to confess. I was mortified at the thought and cried and pleaded with the detective and my husband that there must be another way. I did not want to be alone with that man again. But, I was told it was the only way.

So, a plan was devised whereby the detective told me to call my stepfather at work. He worked at a pectin plant in the middle of nowhere surrounded by fruit grove trees. Once I called him, I was told to tell him that I was seeing a counselor because of the sexual abuse he committed against me for years as a young, underage child and one of the things I had to do as part of my counseling was to confront the person who committed the acts against me. I was to explain to him it was a part of my healing process.

The detective said I would need to make sure he confessed without baiting or luring him into it. He said I just needed to talk until I heard him acknowledge and confess to committing the lewd acts against me. He said I would only have 30 minutes (the guilt had him singing like a bird because it took less than 10 minutes for him to confess) because the small cassette recorder he placed under my sweatshirt would go off after that time, and he would hear it. So, the detective placed the recorder and taped a small microphone to my skin under my clothes. I wore a red sweatshirt with a hood, jeans and white sneakers. He should have realized something was amiss because it was hotter than Hades that day (any day in

Florida feels that way). I was so nervous. Instead of catching a criminal, I suddenly felt like one.

The detective explained he would be parked between the grove trees near my stepfather's job, listening and waiting in the event I was in distress. To say that I was nervous is a gross understatement.

I called my stepfather at work and explained I needed to meet with him. I asked when he would be available, and he said he was glad I had called and that he could be available that afternoon around 1:00 p.m. I told him I'd be there. I called the detective, who said he was available and off we went. The detective turned off into the trees, while I continued to my stepfather's job. I sat anxiously waiting for him to come down the long, paved walkway toward my car. Remembering the smell of his breath became more prominent the closer he got. I was sick to my stomach. When he got closer to my car, I hit the record button on the recorder.

He sat in the passenger seat, and I stared straight ahead and repeated what I was told to say. When I was finished, it took less than five minutes for him to confess and apologize for what he had done. He gave me much more than I needed, and I just let him talk. He said he was glad I called and glad I came and glad I was "seeing someone." He said he probably should do that too because he felt sick for what he had done to me "all that time" and I didn't deserve that. I thanked him and told him I needed to leave. He told me to let me know if there was anything else he could do to help me move beyond the hurt. I sped off, passing the detective who went in the opposite direction to arrest him. He never even made it back to work before he was handcuffed and taken in.

I called my husband and my mother and told them both he was being arrested. Neither of them was surprised, but interestingly enough, they both said that was good for him and that he got what he deserved. They were elated, but I knew I had a long road ahead of me, having to go through the abuse in front of the whole world. I wanted to cower in a corner and just die. It was still so painful.

Things between my husband and I went from bad to worse after that. Now, I understand why. My husband and my mom no longer needed me. I had served them and served them well by removing my stepfather from the equation. I was their cohort in this plan that I knew nothing about. I decided being with him was too much. It was time for me to leave and start my life anew.

So, I called my mother one night to inform her I was going to leave my husband. I told her I was certain he had been unfaithful to me because as I prepared to do laundry that evening, I had found dried up semen on his boxers. It certainly wasn't because we had been intimate, for those days were long gone. Actually, this was one of the things we fought about consistently—the lack of sexual contact. He would say it was because he was tired all the time from work and because I was ten years younger than he.

This could not be further from the truth. As it turns out, there were many female conquests, to include my mother.

During the call to my mother, I informed her I was coming over to her house. I was visibly upset about my decision to leave my husband and wanted to talk with her about it, as I did with everything. She knew every nuance and detail about my marriage, our ups and downs, the ins and outs. She was indeed the third person in my marriage.

When I arrived at my mother's house that night, she had left. I asked one of my sisters who happened to be visiting (this was more than happenstance—more on this later) where our mother had gone. My sister explained that she had gone to Jetson's to pay a bill. I thought that was very strange because she knew I was coming over. I became very restless and began walking robotically to her bedroom. After locking the door behind me, I went to her nightstand and opened the drawer. In it I found, right on top, two Steven Seagal movies. One of them was *Above the Law*. My husband and I had just watched those two movies the night before.

The following day, I had asked him where the movies were because I fell asleep watching them and wanted to watch them again before he took them back to Blockbuster. Mind you, I rarely ask a question for which I don't already know the answer. He responded that it was too late because he had already taken them back. He had not, in fact, taken them back to Blockbuster. He had instead given them to my mother for them to watch together.

I laid the movies on the bed and proceeded to look around her bedroom. I went into the bathroom and looked in her hamper. In it, I found my husband's clothing. He used to work out all the time, so he wore tank tops and sweats when he wasn't working. His tank tops and sweats were in her hamper. In the garbage can were the stems from grapes and empty bottles of Canadian Cleary. He used to eat grapes and drink Canadian Cleary every night before bed. I looked in her drawers where I found more of his clothing. I laid them all on the bed. I performed each action very robotically, unfeeling, without emotion.

I left her bedroom and went back to the family room where my sister sat with her kids and my son. I asked her to come to my mother's bedroom because I had something to show her. Of course, she looked at me quizzically wondering what I could possibly have to show her in our mother's room. I stood at the door before going inside and told her I thought our mother was having an affair with my husband. She stretched her eyes wide and asked me if I had lost my mind because our mother would never do that. I told her I thought the same thing, until this... and I opened the door.

I showed her his clothing, clean and those defiled, I explained the movies and the grapeless stems, along with the emptied water bottles. At nine months pregnant, she took a breath and sat on the edge of the bed, speechless. I asked her to stay with the kids while I took a drive. She asked where I was going, and I told her I needed to find the truth. She went with me while our kids stayed with older siblings.

We drove around for what felt like days. I drove past my mother-in-law's house more times than I can count. I drove past my apartment. I drove through empty parking lots, all while stopping to use various pay phones checking to see if my mother had arrived home so I could end my trek to find her and him. I knew they were together. The feeling wouldn't leave me, even when my sister kept saying it was a wild goose chase and maybe there was some explanation for the things we had discovered in her bedroom. She was trying to make sense of it all like I had done for many, many months. I apologized for bringing her into this mess that had become my life. She just wanted to understand, and so did I.

After finding my husband's truck in an empty parking lot, I told my sister we would go back by my apartment one last time. If they were not there, we would go back to our mother's house and wait. Neither of us could believe it when we pulled up to my apartment to find her vehicle in my parking spot. I told my sister to wait in the car because I wanted to go in quietly. As I entered my apartment, all the lights were off except for the lights in my bedroom, which was in the back of the apartment. I tiptoed to the back, looked around and my sister was following me. I found my mom sitting on the edge of my unmade bed (which was made before I left home) wearing lavender sweatpants and a white shirt, while he was standing in the mirror running his fingers through his hair and drinking red Kool-Aid.

They both saw me at once, and I screamed at my mother, "What are you doing here? What are you doing in my house? In my bed?" She looked as if she had seen a ghost and couldn't speak. All she uttered were gasps. In the meantime, he dropped the Kool-Aid and took off running through the bathroom and out the front door. I was left with her. Needless to say, I was angry that my mother, who was supposed to be at home comforting me, was instead in my bed having sex with my husband. I picked up the lamp and threw it. At the time, I wanted to hurt her like she had hurt me. I did not care that she was my mother, just as she did not care that I was her daughter.

When the lamp missed her, I climbed atop of her and started to hit and hit and hit and hit. My sister pulled me off her, and my mom ran out the door. I got away and ran down the street to find her. I did not know where to find either of them, so I came back to my apartment, fuming. My sister was crying, and I was there to console her. I didn't want to be right, but I was, unfortunately. We went back to my mother's house. Of course, she wasn't there and didn't return home for some time. Someone called my stepfather's brother, who lived down the street and who was a pastor. He came over to pray, but I wasn't having it. I didn't want prayers from the relative of someone who was so vile. Nor did I want to receive prayer at all after such awful things had been done to me.

I worked the night shift at an answering service at the time, so I attempted to clean myself up and go to work. The events of the night had caused me to become so upset that I did not realize I had lost control of my bodily functions. I didn't have a change of clothes, so I rinsed my dress and underwear, showered and left for work.

Shortly after arriving at work, the line rang for Barnett Bail Bonds. To my surprise, when I answered the phone, one of my stepfather's cousins was on the phone explaining she and many of her family members were attempting to get bond for her cousin who had been wrongly accused of molesting some girl. Little did she know, I was the "some girl" she was referencing. Yes, I answered the call and had to reach out to the bondsman on my stepfather's behalf, who was sitting in jail waiting on the response. I could not believe my fate. What sick irony that I was now placed in a position to help get the man out of jail that I had just placed there by virtue of our conversation just hours before.

I could not believe this was happening, and this man was abusing me, indirectly, all over again. I had a duty, so I did for him what I would have done for anyone else seeking a bondsman. I contacted the bondsman to inform him someone wanted to place bail that evening. My job was done. I became ill all over again. I could not escape the torture of it all, and I began to ask myself or tell myself I must have been a horrible person to encounter such occurrences repeatedly. The woman who called the bondsman never even realized she was talking to me, even unto this very day.

Before the end of my shift, I called my mother who, surprisingly, answered my call. I asked her to meet me at my apartment when I got off so we could discuss what happened. I explained I was going to call my husband and invite him to come as well. I just needed to understand. They both agreed to come. He showed up first. She came a short time later. My sister thought I was crazy, but I needed to do it.

When I opened the door and saw her, I hugged her and told her, "I'm sorry." Imagine that, I apologized like I would do so many times in bad relationships, seeking love and approval. I apologized because her nose was broken, and her face was swollen. My heart broke knowing I had done that. I could not believe any of it was happening to me, to us because we had developed a special relationship, or so I thought.

The first question I summoned was "why." I directed it at my mother because I had recently asked her if anything was going on, and she told me "no." I asked her why she tortured me instead of just telling me the truth. Of course, I would have been hurt, but it certainly would not have come to blows because I loved her too much for that.

I asked them both how long their affair lasted. Neither wanted to respond, so they said they weren't sure. I asked them if they loved each other. They looked at each other and then away. I asked if they ever held hands and did inappropriate things in my presence. They didn't respond. It was clear my line of questioning was uncomfortable for them, and I wasn't going to get the answers I was seeking in order to begin my healing process, so I excused them and myself. I explained to my mother that I was heading to her house to collect my son, and I was going to return to my apartment. I knew the calm I felt that day would not last. That was the end of the beginning of a pain that would endure and endure and endure. I would wear that pain like a blanket. In a strange way, the hurt was healing me from the inside out.

I drove around for awhile before heading to my mother's house. Though I had been up all night, I knew I needed to sleep but couldn't; my body wouldn't allow it. I began to process what I would do; how I would begin to heal; how I would care for my son without assistance; and how I would live in this town breathing the same air as the two of them. Anger resurfaced and as quickly as it did, calm returned. I knew I had to think clearly to determine my next steps.

One of my sisters lived in Norfolk, Virginia at the time. Though she and I didn't speak often, I was desperate for help. I needed to leave Vero Beach, Florida for good, and she was my only option, at least temporarily. So, I called her very late that evening and explained the events of the night before. Very tearfully, I asked to impose upon her and her family by living with them for a while until I could land on my feet again. I no longer had sea legs, nice and strong. I was wearing prosthetics that would give way at any given moment. I asked her if she thought my son and I living with her family would cause too much trouble. She said she didn't think so but would check with her husband and give me a call the following day. Of course, she was in utter disbelief.

As promised, she called me the next day to say it would not be a problem for my son and I to live with them temporarily. I was thankful, grateful, elated and sad to be leaving the place where I'd grown up and the place that I had begun to raise my son, but I knew it was the right thing to do. Deep down, I knew he would be better off because I made this decision. Though, I did not tell him right away. I needed to complete the plan first, but knowing I had somewhere to go was the biggest piece to solving the puzzle.

That afternoon, I went to my sister's house and shared with her my plan. I told her I would be going to live with our sister in Norfolk. Of course, she was emotional, and so was I. After we dried our tears, we planned the next steps. I needed to figure out how to get to Virginia, so we decided the bus would be the most cost-effective way for transportation. I went to Barnett Bank to withdraw all the funds from our account, only to learn my husband had almost drained our account. There was only $134 left in it, so I withdrew that, went back to my car and cried because I knew that was not nearly enough for two bus tickets.

I went back to my sister's apartment to share the news. I became a recluse at her house, only coming out at night because I didn't want my husband to see me, and I didn't want to cause problems for my sister and her family. I just wanted to leave and forget the events of the last few days had ever happened. We put our heads together and decided I would sell everything from my apartment and whatever was left, my sister would take it. She began calling all her friends to purchase televisions, furniture, and everything and anything else of value. Finally, we collected enough money to purchase the bus tickets and have a little left over for food.

Our bus was due to depart a couple of days later. Since I had sold nearly everything from my apartment, my son and I stayed at my sister's house until my bus was due to leave. My husband would come to my sister's house on more than one occasion asking if I was there. Every time my sister would tell him I wasn't and every time, he would tell her to ask me to call him. I never did.

When the day arrived for us to leave, as my sister took us to the bus station, we passed my husband again heading to my sister's house to see if I was there. My sister waited with us until the bus arrived and until it left the station. That was one of the saddest days of my life. I was going to miss her dearly because she saved my life. My sister said my husband showed up one last time after she got home from the bus station, and she finally told him I had left town. He never showed up again.

I knew my son and I were headed for new beginnings, but I was so afraid of the unknown. I was taking my child from a familiar place to a place so unfamiliar. My son was a trooper, always so quiet with such a peaceful disposition. He quietly held my hand, and my tears just flowed. In that moment, my son gave me the kind of strength, the kind of resolve I would need for the rest of my life. He has always been so wise. He was now my priority. I was responsible for him, and I refused to allow him to see a weak woman. No, he would see a woman who would rise from the pain and turmoil into someone he would always be proud of and a woman he would use to measure as the barometer for his future wife. He needed to see that storms will come, and you can never be prepared with a life raft for them all, but you can *create* a life raft in any given circumstance to see the sun rise the next day.

I made the decision to move to Norfolk after I realized my mother and husband were in cahoots to remove my stepfather from the picture. It was then that I decided I had been used enough. I could not understand how my mother could use my pain to cause even more pain to satisfy her own desires. Sure, my husband played a role, but he was not blood. She should have known better and done better. Instead, she became an active participant with my husband in using me, no matter the cost, no matter the outcome for me.

By virtue of moving to Virginia and never pursuing the case, I dropped the charges against my stepfather. Some have questioned why the case was never brought against my father and why he was exonerated. Well now, a whole lot of those inquiring minds know. He was not exonerated because he was innocent; he was exonerated because of that day when the muted little girl decided to take her innocence back, and she did it in the biggest way possible. She took her power by standing her ground and walking away by taking a long bus ride from Florida to Virginia, her first time ever leaving the state, the only she'd ever known. This moment, writing her story, is how she decided her power would best be exercised and exercise it, did she.

It was a very long bus ride, but we made it to Norfolk. I even managed to get on and off the bus at the right locations, even in the dead of night in suspect locations. It was terrifying. We didn't have much, so that made the load a little lighter. My sister and her husband and two kids picked us up from the bus station. It was so good to see them. We had not seen each other in years. I thanked them for picking us up and for allowing us to live in their home for a while.

My sister and I did not discuss what happened right away, but when we did, she could hardly believe it. She had conflicting emotions because she always wanted to be the "fixer" and repairer of wrongs. This time, her rose-colored glasses reflected crimson. She promised to do what she could to support me in my healing. She and the kids showed us around the house and the neighborhood. They lived on a military base in Norfolk which felt like a fortress to us.

Of course, I didn't have a job or money when I arrived, so I applied for public assistance until I could find a job. Fortunately, I received it fairly quickly, and the food stamps allowed me to help with groceries. As kids do, her kids and my son didn't always get along. My son said the two of them would gang up on him and not give him a snack after school. So, the easiest remedy was to stash snacks in our bedroom so he would have something to snack on when I wasn't at home. I didn't want conflict because we needed a place to live.

Shortly after arriving in Norfolk, I received a call from my grandmother. She was crying and was clearly devastated. When I asked what was wrong, she explained that my mother was going around town telling anyone who asked about me that she had me committed to the "crazy house" because I thought she was having an affair with my husband. My grandmother said, "Lenny, you're not crazy. She was sleeping with your husband and everybody around town knew it." I told her I knew that was the case but had moved on and was now living in Norfolk trying to get back on my feet. I assured her I was fine and had not been committed anywhere. When she felt certain that was the case, we ended our call. I was furious at my mother because rather than acknowledge what she had done, she wanted to further humiliate and disparage me by saying I was crazy. I was so angry!

Not long after arriving in Norfolk, I found out I was pregnant. I couldn't understand why I was sick all the time and having uncontrollable headaches. I wasn't eating and still felt nauseous. I went to the clinic, and to my surprise, I was two months pregnant. I could not imagine enduring all the things I had in addition to learning my husband and mother were having an affair, moving to a new city in another state with no money, no place of my own to live and the ongoing list of "I don't have..."

I endured yet another bad decision on my own and chose to abort this child. I never even told my husband I was pregnant, nor did I tell my mother. Only my sister and I knew. That was good enough for me. I think about that child and what his or her life would be like. I often wonder why I chose to abort that child but never wanted to abort the life of my son. Only God knows why things happen as they do. This decision caused me to look at myself differently. The new stain I labeled myself: murderer with an unborn child's blood on my hands. The picture wasn't a pretty one, and the tapestry looked uglier by the day.

My then-husband tried contacting me many times, and I finally spoke with him over the phone. He asked if I was returning home, and my response was a hearty laugh. He threatened that if I didn't return home he would file for divorce. "Great," was my response, "because then I won't have to." Months later, I received divorce papers in the mail because in the state of Florida, once one party files and the other person does not respond within 30 days, the divorce or annulment is automatic. Our marriage was annulled. Case and chapter closed.

Before I started working, I would walk the kids to school and meet them after school. I lost so much weight by doing that, I went from a size 16 to a size 8 in a short time. I was stressed about not working. I was stressed about not having my own home. I was stressed about not having a car. I was just stressed, and there didn't seem to be an end to my stress in sight until one day, I received a child support check from the Child Support Enforcement office in Florida. It was almost $4,000, which was more than enough to get an apartment and pay utilities, but it was not enough to purchase furniture.

So, I saved the money and eventually found a job, two of them. I relied on my sister to get me from one job to the next job and would give her money for gas. At times, she could not come to pick me up, so I would walk on I-64 to get from my day job to my evening job. I would leave my evening job just after midnight to get home, sleep a few hours and do it all over again. Those were extremely difficult times, but they were necessary. I didn't realize how much I didn't know until I didn't know what I didn't know. I was traveling down a road with people all around me, and yet, I could not have felt more alone. The road my feet were trodding was beyond difficult. There were so many twists and turns, and my feet were becoming more and more worn. I deserved it for all the damage my life had caused. I just wanted the best for my son; my life didn't matter all that much.

The lack of maternal warmth and validation from my mother began to warp my sense of self and the manner in which I viewed other relationships. I lacked self-confidence and was extremely wary of close emotional connections, which shaped and reshaped those connections in ways that were both seen and unseen. Unlike the daughter who may be unadulteratedly and unapologetically loved, I was the daughter of an unattuned mother, so I did not grow up in the reflected rays of sunlight. Rather, I felt like the unloved daughter diminished by virtue of this wicked connection with my mother. Though I still feel the pains of being unloved, it is true those sentiments are very much the same for me today. They have not wavered. Why? Because the elephant remains in the room. Conversations that should have taken place years ago have gone unspoken. Love, lost. Wounds, unhealed. Hurt, mirrored.

Somewhere along the way, and for a reason I have yet to understand, my relationship with my mother shifted.

Our roles seemed to change from that of mother-daughter before the molestation to sister-sister when we'd hang out on the weekends and close girlfriends when I met my husband. My mother's desire to be in a relationship with my husband distorted her role in my life, and her distorted view caused her to become emotionally unavailable to me and for me. I suppose she was always unavailable after the molestation by my stepfather, but the transition was more difficult to notice because as a little girl, you just want to be noticed, period.

I believed she had an affair with my then-husband because of the disgusting and perverse relationship her ex-husband chose to have with a very young girl, her daughter, the daughter she never even bothered to protect. I believe she did it because she resented the fact that this pedophile chose to affect his vile behavior upon me. In her eyes, I suppose she feels he chose me over her. Whatever the reason, it was wrong, and it was a choice. A mistake happens only once, but to actively engage in a situation multiple times becomes a choice. Even after I left Florida and moved to Virginia, they continued to see each other. So, to hurt me, she chose my ex-husband over me. She chose revenge over love.

So much was happening during this time, and I must admit that much of what occurred escapes me, and for good measure. It is deeply hurtful and egregious because the pain of my wounds is borne from the hands of a mother's love. Yes, quite the conundrum, I know.

I recall when one of my sisters questioned me about what my stepfather may or may not have been doing to me. She said she would kill him if she ever learned what was going on. I was scared to death. I didn't know whether to tell the truth or a lie. So, I lied. I told her "no."

I did so for many reasons, but the main reason was because my stepfather reminded me of when my brother tried to tell my mother what happened. My mother didn't believe him and kicked him out of the house. He promised me I would meet with the same fate, only I would have nowhere to go and nowhere to live because nobody would want me. I would be labeled as a troublemaker. So, I took his perverse hands and stinky breath for years to come. Those were the most horrific days of my life.

My mother actively withdrew from me for a time after the molestation, and I felt she withheld love from one child while granting it to others, inflicting a different kind of damage. Because of evolution, all children are hardwired to rely on their mothers. My mother was not a mean person, by any stretch of the imagination, especially to those not living in our home. No, she was not mean; she was emotionally disconnected from me and still is.

There were times since the turmoil of my childhood that I would do things to prove to her I could and did so without her help. I wanted to prove she didn't break me and that I moved on from the hurt she and my stepfather and ex-husband caused. The damage was severe and lots of carnage was left in the wake. I was ripped to shreds and had no idea how to begin to become whole again. I had a son and knew I had to do whatever it took to make sure he would be better than okay.

I even continued to buy my mother really nice birthday and Christmas gifts to prove a point. Then, I thought, what really is the point of it all? I'm not doing these things out of love for my mother; I was doing them out of obligation. So, I grew up. I stopped doing it. I just stopped because it no longer served me well to pretend. It was a heavy burden lifted that I no longer needed to carry. The act of actively participating in these things was so disingenuine.

I felt the sting of her abandonment through lack of physical contact (no hugging, no comforting); unresponsiveness or no display of emotion and, of course, literal abandonment. I was mentally, emotionally, spiritually and physically abandoned, which left their own scars, scars so indelibly etched throughout my mind and body, they promised me they'd never leave. I was stuck with all those ugly, nasty scars for a lifetime. This was especially pervasive because of the culture which believes in the automatic nature of a mother's love and instinctual behavior.

In addition to being excruciatingly painful, it was also bewildering sorting through many of these issues trying to decide what I needed to keep and what needed to be thrown out. Sifting through this part of my life made it unbelievably difficult because the void that remained during the sifting process was huge, and I only wanted my mom to fill it with apologies and promises it would be okay because she would never leave my side again.

Bishop Noel Jones once said you should never commit yourself to someone or make decisions when you're extremely high or extremely low because when things begin to settle in, you wake up one day and wonder how you got there. I allowed someone to choose me at a very, very low point in my life. My vulnerability would become a magnet for broken relationships.

God, the eraser of my guilty stains of single motherhood spoke to me in Matthew 10:35-36 and said:

35"For I have come to turn a man against his father, a daughter against her mother, a daughter-in-law against her mother-in-law— 36a man's enemies will be the members of his own household."

I saw my mother as my enemy. She betrayed me in the worst way possible. Instead of giving, she took. And the void that would remain continued to take in many says. I could not look to another soul. Isolation became my very best friend. It felt good to isolate because I did not fear the hurt again. I sat with the hurt, the pain and the guilt, and rocked it to sleep on many nights. Or at least, I'd like to think the story was read that way; however, the hurt, the pain and the guilt mostly rocked me—to my core, the deepest parts of me. I felt unlovable.

As time moved on, so did the eraser. The stains became less prominent, and I slowly poked my head out from my shell like a turtle checking the environment before feeling it was safe to come out again. When it felt quasi safe, I began to unravel the dark places by removing the stains, one-by-one.

Removal of the Stain of a Mother's Betrayal

Betrayal of any kind leaves us with two choices: we can choose to allow the betrayal to grow us or allow it to stunt our growth. I chose to grow through the betrayal and pain it caused in every area of my life. The betrayal provided countless lessons and invaluable wisdom for my path forward.

Here's how:

1. I had to erase the stains, the imprints of the **betrayal**. Almost daily, I had to be intentional in extracting the wounds from my subconscious mind. They were always right at the surface, threatening to destroy. To ease these thoughts, I meditated early and often. I wrote and cried. Writing became therapeutic ; it helped me to remember and to forget. There is so much beauty in it. Writing became clearer for me and my view became less obstructed because of it. I replayed the words from my Father that I must honor my mother so that my days would be long. As much as I recalled that scripture, I wondered where was my mother's honor for me. Why was it lost ? Why was I betrayed so deeply ? As quickly as the questions arose, I realized I would likely never receive the answer(s) I was seeking, so for self-

preservation's sake, I dismissed those questions. Instead, I focused on who my Father proclaimed of me in His word.

2. I chose to **forgive** knowing that forgiveness didn't mean reconciliation. I knew (and accepted) that my relationship with my mother would never again be the same. Even now, I do not sense the genuineness in our conversations ; they are very sterile. Acknowledging that this relationship with my mother would likely be our new normal was a major hurdle for me because I truly lost my best friend, or so I thought. The best friend I envisioned was the one that listened to my cares and the concerns of my heart and would protect them with her life; my shopping buddy ; and the person with whom I thought had moved beyond the molestation and was walking with me, albeit out of guilt, to a peaceful place. As it turned out, I had to truly forgive and dismiss the notion that she had planned this whole debacle of switching roles from that of mother to mistress, from start to finish, without bothering to clue me in. Memories are really a blessing and a curse, especially in this case because the memory of the stain makes it that much harder to erase.

Creating images and actually remembering an actual visual are two entirely different things. I continued to recall the visual images of him and her in my apartment. While those images and the realization of what occurred between the two of them was etched in my mind, forgiveness was my only pathway through the pain; forgetting would be a different story altogether.

3. I kept a **journal** of the emotions that arose from the betrayal and how they triggered certain behaviors. I wrote and wrote and wrote. This act began the process of my healing. I would go back often and read some of my journals, and when they no longer hurt the way they did when I first began writing, I knew that I was okay. The worst of the storm was behind me. My legs no longer felt like they were laden with cement boulders.

4. I allowed my **faith** to flourish again. I was so angry and so hurt for so long. I wasn't consciously aware of blaming God for all that happened to me, but as I have grown stronger in my faith and in my love for Him, I realized that I absolutely did blame Him. I just could not imagine anything good resulting from such a

horrible childhood. I found grace, peace, solace, wisdom, clarity and a lot of rest in His open arms.

5. I **grieved** the lost relationship with my mother and allowed myself to be okay with that. When my daughter was born, I was in Okinawa, Japan. I always envisioned my mother there with me for the birth of my second child, and yet, it would be years before she even met my daughter, her granddaughter. I often blamed myself because of the disconnect between my daughter and her grandmother, but I have come to understand that people create their own priorities, and that has absolutely nothing to do with me.

6. I allowed myself to **feel** what my mother must have been feeling. I knew that there had to be some part of her that was grieving for me, just as much as I was grieving for her. Even though the betrayal ran deep and stretched wide, she still gave birth to me. How could she not feel some semblance of grief and guilt for her part in the betrayal ?

7. Once I found my faith in Christ again, I began to **believe** in myself again. This didn't come easy and doubt became the twin sister to my faith. Like a child learning to ride a bike, I didn't forget, but it was a lot harder getting back on the bike after falling down so hard. It was necessary to trust myself again and to believe in relationships, tried and true relationships again.

8. I had to be open to **love** again in every way. I thank God every single day these experiences didn't cause me to be jaded by love. I struggled (and still do) with trusting other people. One day, I realized I cannot survive in this world alone and not giving others an opportunity to know what it is like to love me and to be in relationship with me, was not God's best for me. To refuse love was denying myself of His greatest gift for my life. So much had already been taken from me; I was bound and determined not to allow love to escape my grasp. So, I opened myself up... to more broken relationships.

"People have to pretend you're a bad person, so they don't feel guilty for what they did to you."

~ Anonymous

GS 4

The Stain of Broken Relationships

*"I asked her if she believed in love, and she smiled and
said it was her most elaborate method of self-harm."*
~ Benedict Smith

My, how I longed for the sound of my father's voice
in those days, weeks and months after my mother's
betrayal. I wondered what he would have thought, what
he would have said or if it would have happened at all. I
needed to hear him tell me I was enough, and the
decisions I made, and choices made by others, even those
closest to me did not define me. I yearned to hear his voice
of protection for his little girl. I wanted him to sweep me
up into his arms, wrap me in a loving embrace and remind
me that true love exists, even in pain because pain always
has a purpose. I imagined him speaking to me and that
imagination would serve to get me through the darkest of
nights. I didn't remember what his voice sounded like, but
I imagined, and that was good enough.

When I left Florida and moved to Virginia, I felt as though I was walking through clouds every day. Fantasy became reality for me again. I couldn't even imagine what the next day would bring, day after day. One Saturday night, my sister, her husband and the kids were preparing to go bowling. My sister's husband had a friend come by to go with them. This friend was in the military, serving alongside my brother-in-law in the United States Marine Corps. He was in town taking classes as a condition of their service at the time. He urged me to go with them, and of course, I continued to refuse. Though I didn't know my type, I knew for sure he wasn't it. I was not even remotely attracted to him, yet, he continued to pursue me. They left for the bowling alley, and just as I was getting settled for an evening alone, the phone rang. It was my brother-in-law's friend urging me to come. He promised to pick me up and leave me alone once we got there if I didn't want to be bothered. I relented. I got dressed, and he returned to pick me up.

We went on several dates after that night. I still didn't feel an electric chemistry or a longing for this relationship. Even still, I actively participated. I allowed myself to give in to what this man wanted instead of stepping back, realizing my vulnerability and refusing to settle. Looking back, I didn't know what "enough" was, so how could I possibly know that I was enough? I did not have the luxury of knowing yet what I wanted in a relationship because Mr. Example didn't show up for me.

On one of our dates, this man shared with me that his wife and he were separated; they had two small kids together. Why didn't I flee at those words? Why didn't I realize that God would never have sent me a married man, no matter how "separated" they were? He would never bring me happiness at the expense of someone else's pain. This man said all the right things, like, "God sent me here to rescue you." Oh, really? Why couldn't I see through to the fact that this was not God?

Instead, it was a dangling carrot, and I was hungry. Hungry for what? I didn't know. There was an incredibly large void in my life that left me empty, but I didn't know what I wanted to eat. Nothing was appealing to me, especially not this man. There was something about him I knew wasn't right, but maybe over time... I could not have been more wrong. He was controlling, and after experiencing betrayal and molestation, I moved with the flow. It was second nature. He partially filled a void, and I accepted.

He lived in North Carolina, so I would go visit him on the weekends with my son, but I could tell immediately he didn't really like my child. I believed he was so angry that his own boys didn't live with us, he would take it out on my child. He wouldn't allow my son to play with any of his boys' toys. He wouldn't spend time with him, and yet, I accepted this.

I actually moved in with him before we were married, an act I would live to regret for a very long time. It was hard finding a job because I didn't have a lot of experience, nor did I have a college degree, which he would remind me of often. So, I relied on him for quite some time, and with his controlling nature, it was the prescription to aid his controlling nature and the need to feel authoritative. I depended on him for everything my son and I needed.

When I wasn't working, I prepared three hot meals for him each day. When I finally started working every check went to him. I had no idea how much he earned, but he added my meager wages to it. I did what I thought I was supposed to do, just wanting my life to be better. I thought he helped in that regard, so I didn't want to do anything to cause him to leave me.

I can recall an instance when he decided to purchase new living room furniture. Not only did he select the furniture on his own, but when the delivery men came, he sent my son and I to the park so that he could have it set up without interruption or distraction. He said he would let us know when we could come back to the house. It was hours later in the heat that my son and I were sitting under a gazebo waiting to go home. I felt humiliated, like a child, but again, I accepted it.

He received orders to go overseas, and since we were not married, I could not go. He set the wheels in motion to divorce his wife and marry me so that I could go with him. Had I been in my right mind, I would not have entered into what should have been a lifelong commitment so hurriedly. After his divorce was final, we began making rapid plans to get married. With our marriage license in hand, we went to WalMart, purchased rings and proceeded to the courthouse in New Bern, North Carolina to get married. My gut was screaming out. Even in the certainty of my uncertainty, I moved forward with the marriage. The officiator recruited two individuals working in his office to stand as our witnesses since we didn't bring anyone with us. As we stood in the judges' chambers with two perfectly willing strangers, we said our "I do's." Why did I willfully engage in hurriedly running to a burning altar? Why did I say "I do" when I clearly didn't?

This broken relationship did its best to break me, and it nearly did. Instead, it led me into the path of a church with a pastor who would help me to understand what the Bible actually says about love and divorce. Don't get me wrong, the pastor was not a proponent of divorce, but he stood up from behind his foreboding desk, sat down next to me, took my hand and said he wanted to introduce me to a spiritual counselor to talk with me about my past and my present. He said if a relationship isn't a reflection of God's love, then we must ask ourselves if the relationship is of God or of flesh. He was quick to add that even though sometimes we choose relationships ourselves without God's blessing, it doesn't mean He won't bless it; however, it does mean that both parties must be willing to seek His blessing. He also read to me what God says about love. I can recite it verbatim because I would recall it time and time again.

God says in Ephesians 5:25-28, *25 "For husbands, this means love your wives, just as Christ loved the church. He gave up his life for her 26 to make her holy and clean, washed by the cleansing of God's word.[a] 27 He did this to present her to himself as a glorious church without a spot or wrinkle or any other blemish. Instead, she will be holy and without fault. 28 In the same way, husbands ought to love their wives as they love their own bodies. For a man who loves his wife actually shows love for himself."*

And another in 1 Corinthians 13:4-7, *4 "Love is patient and kind. Love is not jealous or boastful or proud 5 or rude. It does not demand its own way. It is not irritable, and it keeps no record of being wronged. 6 It does not rejoice about injustice but rejoices whenever the truth wins out. 7 Love never gives up, never loses faith, is always hopeful, and endures through every circumstance."*

Neither of these scriptures represented love in my marriage. The funny thing is my husband would constantly recite the portion of scripture that says a wife should submit to her husband, but interestingly enough, he couldn't remember his responsibility about loving his wife as Christ loved the church. And so, he didn't.

After counseling and getting stronger and believing what God said about me instead of what my husband said about me, I decided it was time to leave. I had very little money at the time, so I asked him to file for divorce. At first, he refused to do it and decided that buying a $550,000 house would solve our problems. It didn't.

He went overseas after purchasing the house and expected that all would be so very different while he was away. He was right, to a degree. I was different. I no longer accepted the charity he wished to lend my way. I no longer believed this was all there was in relationships. I no longer believed I needed to settle for the "bird in my hand." What was exceedingly different was my mindset, and I attribute the evolution to prayer and building healthy relationships apart from my husband. I realized that I had been settling into a relationship that was comfortable. No, not comfortable in the sense that it was enjoyable, but comfortable in the sense of the known versus the unknown.

I allowed myself to begin thinking about "what if." What if there was another man out there who was created especially for me? What if he was waiting for me to get the strength to come to him? What if there wasn't? What if I left him and another man wasn't waiting to find me? What if I made the decision to leave and remained alone the rest of my life? For a moment, that last "what if" excited me a bit. I know that sounds strange. Who really wants to be alone? I decided in that moment that actually being alone had to be far better than feeling alone while in a dead-end relationship that offered nothing short of loneliness day in and day out. The thought of him returning home didn't excite me. I knew then it was time to exit the marriage.

Shortly after he came back from overseas, my husband and I legally separated, and I moved on, never thinking I would look back. I began dating again, if you can call it that. I began seeing a man, who, unfortunately, was still married. I was so broken, I didn't know what right felt like, but this wasn't it. Oh, I really liked him; I was smitten and so was he. Again, we both eventually filled a void for each other. Because we were both still married, the relationship wasn't free. We weren't free to see each other as we would have liked. Because of my legal separation, I was unencumbered while he was not.

Eventually, his wife and my soon-to-be-ex would learn of our relationship. My husband hired a private investigator to follow us around. We both knew it because we would see the same guy within feet from us driving the same dark SUV with tinted windows. We both laughed it off. What was the point of it all? By this time, I didn't care. There was nothing my husband could take from me that I hadn't already given away.

The man I was seeing worked on the military base, so my husband pulled rank and told his superiors that he was having an affair with his wife. All hell broke loose, and the man was fired from his job immediately. My boss, who I loved dearly, called me into the office and shared what happened. My job was safe, but after the disaster and everyone learning of what happened, I applied for another job in Wilmington, North Carolina and moved away.

I hoped the man would leave his wife and join me, but he chose to remain with her. I was devastated but had to face the consequences of my own actions and move on with my life. The pain of it all was as fresh as raindrops that fall from a sunny sky. You just don't expect it; you absorb the raindrops, allow them to dry and change your own outlook.

I continued to hope he would call and tell me he had a change of heart, but I wouldn't hear from him for many years. He was actually the man who encouraged me to reconnect with my mother after her betrayal. He contacted me several years ago, and we were able to finally talk and close the door to the past. We acknowledged our personal pain and how my ex-husband's actions affected who we were back then. It didn't change us, but it definitely impacted us and who we were. One thing I loved about our relationship was how he was so unafraid to talk about his feelings, and he did so through letters and emails because he wanted me to have something tangible on which to reflect when we weren't together. In one of those letters, he told me that I was a caged bird who didn't realize her wings were for flying. I never forgot that.

There were a couple of relationships after this one that lead me to my current relationship. I dated a man for about two years, and he was my epiphany. I'm sure he doesn't realize it, but he was the man that helped me realize that I was needy. I was choosing relationships based on my need to be loved. I wanted it desperately, so I felt the more I did, the more love I gave, maybe I would be loved just as much in return. Love just doesn't happen that way. What I learned from that relationship is that love and hurt don't belong in the same sentence. Love does. Love is. Love gives. Love does not hurt.

Broken relationships chased me down. I was a magnet for them, even with girlfriends. I gave, and they often took without a backwards glance or giving in return. But as I think about those relationships, I know now that I didn't give very much either. I gave pieces of me that I knew would heal fastest if the wounds cut deeply enough. I guarded the secret places I knew that, if opened, they would erupt like a volcano holding onto lava for many years. I drew on fantasy from my childhood a lot. It was the thing I was good at. I was good at designing masks for every situation. A girlfriend betrays my trust and breaks my confidence because she's angry with me. I had a mask for that. A family member breaks away and sides with other family members against me. I had a mask for that. There was no mask that didn't fit every situation perfectly until... they just didn't.

Healing from broken relationships is always tough, but it is even tougher to heal when you don't know if the relationship requires healing or walking away altogether. Broken relationships had me questioning everything I once believed was true. I wondered why it wasn't happening for me. The "it" being love. Why wasn't it happening for me like it was for the people who I felt didn't deserve it. I wondered why I had to suffer from broken relationships long before I even knew what a relationship was.

The molestation gave me a very unrealistic view of relationships—healthy or unhealthy, real or imagined. The relationship with my stepfather would become the only real barometer I had to measure love or what it meant to be in any relationship, especially one of torment with someone. Maybe this kind of abuse was right because after all, my mother married him and brought him into our lives. So, I thought, my mother loved me, and if she could love him enough to bring him into our lives, it must be okay.

I would quickly learn this wasn't the case at all because love didn't feel like my fantasy. The older I got and the longer the abuse continued, the more I realized this wasn't right. This is not how love was supposed to feel. It couldn't be because it hurt too much. Love wasn't supposed to hurt or at least that is what I would hear the preacher say almost every Sunday. That is the part I remembered most. It has surely stuck with me for most of my life. There are very few things in life that compare with the satisfaction and joy and connectedness that comes when we're deeply loved and when we love deeply in authentic, meaningful relationships.

As I thought about life's ups and downs and everything I had been through, starting with the molestation, one of the greatest things I ever wanted to taste on this earth is that deep, authentic, abiding connection where someone loved me for me. Not for what I had, not for what I could do, not for where I'd been, not for who I knew, but because he just loved me, and it was reciprocal because I loved him too.

By contrast, few things in this life will ever hurt as badly and as deeply as the wounds and sorrow and the alienation that comes when a relationship is broken, especially between mother and daughter. Can two hearts ever heal from it? It wasn't just romantic relationships that suffered, it was also platonic relationships that met a demise because once fractured, no matter the reason, they would heal, but the limb would never be the same. The limb is almost like that of a phantom limb, where you know the limb isn't there, but you still feel the sensation from it. Whether it be pain, strength or weakness, the emotion still holds on long after the limb is either gone or just doesn't work or heal the way you would hope. That is the story of my life with relationships that began and ended exactly the same, fracturing in the same spot over and over. You never really heal from broken relationships; the hurt just hurts less. The memory of the pain, the memory of the stain lasts forever.

I needed some way to cope. Again, I went to the one thing that was my source of strength for every circumstance, the Bible. Because of my deep faith in him I did not have to search long. Here are four Bible verses my

God, the eraser of my guilty stains, gave me to cope. These verses helped me to remember I wasn't alone.

1. **Practice Humility**: "Be always humble, gentle, and patient. Show your love by being tolerant with one another." (Ephesians 4:2)

2. **Offer Forgiveness**: "Instead, be kind and tender-hearted to one another, and forgive one another, as God has forgiven you through Christ." (Ephesians 4:32)

3. **Communicate Authentically**: "Remember this, my dear friends! Everyone must be quick to listen, but slow to speak and slow to become angry." (James 1:19)

4. **Exercise Patience**: "Let your hope keep you joyful, be patient in your troubles, and pray at all times." (Romans 12:12)

Remembering these four verses allowed me to move forward and alter the way I engaged in relationships. To move forward, I had to go back. I knew that I must remove this stain in order to experience healthy and whole relationships.

Removal of the Stain of Broken Relationships

1. I began to live life on my own terms, no excuses and no apologies.

2. Compromising for the sake of compromising was no longer an option.

3. I learned to be present and free in every single moment, especially from the past hurts and disappointments of my life.

4. I began to speak with conviction, courageously sharing my thoughts, feelings and ambitions with the people in my life who truly cared for me and my well-being.

5. I spoke affirmations and words of encouragement over my life daily.

6. I forgave myself for accepting less than God's best for me.

7. I allowed myself to feel the pain, with no apologies. Strangely, feeling the pain, not reveling in it, brought me back to life so many times before.

8. I stopped blaming my mother for every failed relationship. Sure, she played her part, but I realized I was playing roles that were never created for me. So, instead of being the understudy, I promoted myself to leading lady for every decision and every consequence.

9. I allowed myself time to heal and reflected often on the things I needed in relationship and the things I

needed to dismiss long before entertaining them. I felt my human spirit coming to life again.

10. I had to remember not to betray others because betrayal happened to me. I refused to knowingly deceive or mislead others to satisfy my pain. Revenge only perpetuates bad karma and traps you in a cycle of recurring action.

11. I regained trust in others slowly but was intentional and rational in my level of trust toward others. I placed my hopes in loved ones that taught me that yes, there still exists goodhearted people in whom I could confide.

12. Learning to control my emotions remains a challenge for me. I realize my emotions can be your best friend or your worst enemy. They are the essence of our existence, but when they're taken to the extreme, they can downright block our lives. We can easily become stuck in our feelings, mentally and even physically. In order to heal from betrayal and keep it from reoccurring in the future, I must keep my emotions in check. There is no optionality in that. Obsessing over something that happened in the past causes me to become stuck in that moment in time. Thinking logically and understanding the need to move forward allowed me to master my emotions. I am still very much a work in progress.

13. I renewed my faith in God and remembered how He made a way for me so many times before. God loves

me with an everlasting love and nobody on this earth can love me better. Remembering how God loves me would become the ultimate test for migrating through failed and successful relationships. He would do the same this time and heal my broken heart many times over.

GS 5

The Stain of Divorce

"The price of anything is the amount of life you exchange for it."
                                        ~ *Henry David Thoreau*

I will never forget the day I decided. It was a Sunday, and I wasn't feeling well. I stayed home from church and watched *Eat, Pray, Love* with Julia Roberts. Watching this movie for the first time while lying in my bed with a box of Kleenex was a defining moment for me. There was a line (actually, there were many of them) when Julia says, "I'm choosing happiness over suffering, I know I am. I'm making space for the unknown future to fill up my life with yet-to-come surprises." In another scene, she talks about loneliness. She says, "When I get lonely these days, I think, 'So *be* lonely, Liz. Learn your way around loneliness. Make a map of it. Sit with it for once in your life. Welcome to the human experience. But never again use another person's body or emotions as a scratching post for your own unfulfilled yearnings.'" It was time.

There were many relationships I had built during this challenging time. When we moved to Stafford, Virginia and I began working at a hospital in the area, I formed a relationship with my manager at the time that I have maintained. She was and is a strong woman of faith. We had so much in common. We both have sons who have broken or non-existent relationships with their fathers, and we both lived in North Carolina for a time. Our relationship was divinely providential. I shared with her almost immediately the struggles I was having in my marriage. She was there, always there, sharing in my tears along with many talks, many, many ups and downs and much, much uncertainty.

When I finally shared with her I was divorcing my husband, while she was glad I had found some relief and peace in making this decision, she was also saddened by the long road ahead. The only way I could afford an attorney was to liquidate some of my retirement funds, but I told my friend/manager and my pastor that I didn't believe this was the right direction. I didn't know why I felt the way I did, but I didn't believe God would send me through this divorce only to leave me broken and broke. They both thought I was nuts not to hire an attorney. I had to go with what God placed in my spirit, which was to go it alone.

My husband served me with divorce papers through the mail even though we both lived under the same roof (except I lived in the one bedroom, fully furnished and fully functional basement). The only time I glimpsed him was when I was preparing dinner for my daughter and me. Other than that, I never saw him.

Now, years before, my husband and I separated legally. I signed over everything to him—the house, his military retirement, all of it because I had no intentions of ever going back. Big mistake! After his urging and pleading and telling me he had seen the light and the error of his ways and how he just wanted his family back, I left the life I was building with my kids and went back. After all, I thought, why shouldn't I go back if he really had turned his life over to God. Again, *bigger* mistake.

Within six months, he was treating me the exact same way he did before I left. The only difference this time was the legal separation papers I signed one year before were still valid. I had forgotten all about it, but he hadn't, which is why he refused to share anything with me.

This became crystal clear when I received the divorce papers. The first thing his attorney noted was that I was not entitled to his retirement. The house, however, belonged to us both, and the only way he could sell was for me to sign it over. Even though my name was not on the mortgage, it was on the deed. That was God looking out for me long before I knew it. The house would be the insurance policy I never knew I had.

To say that my soon-to-be-ex was angry and bitter that I chose to leave him was a gross understatement. I had the audacity to not only ask for the divorce but to ask him to go file because I knew he'd have to pay the court costs. That was more money I did not have in liquidated cash. I had done enough research to know that.

He did his best to break me into tiny little pieces, pieces so tiny they could never be whole again. I remember him telling me to get out of his house, and if I did so that day, he would give me $1,500. I told him I'd take my chances in court because what I knew for sure is that what was for Lynn was absolutely for Lynn. This man could not take it away from me.

I was stressed to the max because I needed an attorney, but the cheapest divorce attorney informed me I would need to pay him $15,000 to represent me in court and that he could offer no promises that I would even get that money back in the divorce because of the separation agreement I signed.

Now, mind you, this attorney, who was referred to me by my then-pastor, wanted desperately to help me because of his relationship with my pastor and, in fact, had attended court with me once before at no charge. He called me the night before my first court appearance saying he wanted to help me as a courtesy to my pastor. He did this without even knowing anything about my case, but he trusted my pastor and therefore, trusted me. Talk about the hand and grace of God.

After the attorney read the separation agreement that I poured over, line-by-line, he came to a section about child support. He asked me if my husband had ever paid me child support during our legal separation. I replied, "no." The attorney promptly returned my separation agreement to me and instructed me to take it to my local Child Support Enforcement office because my husband owed me for child support over a 10-year period. Again, the grace of God and another insurance policy I knew nothing about. My husband was not only ordered by the court to pay a large sum in delinquent child support, but he was ordered to continue paying child support until our daughter turned 18, which was two years away... another insurance policy.

My husband was livid. He called me every name under the sun—at least that is what I learned through others because he never had the courage to say those things to me. He went to my church and accused my pastor and me of having an affair. He met with church deacons; his sister called the church office; and the lies continued. He never wanted me to continue going to the church that provided me with free counseling and a group of women who would become my covering. This church family gathered around me like never before. With the exception of the pastor, only a few knew of my circumstances at home.

For the first time, I felt like it was okay to move forward without my husband. I often say that it is okay to be vulnerable, just make sure those around you can handle your vulnerability. That was not the case with my husband because when he finally realized what he stood to lose, he began telling anyone and everyone who would listen that I was the product of molestation by my stepfather, and I was wounded. He tried warning other men that because I was so broken, I could not be in a healthy relationship.

This was the lowest of the low, however, I had to keep moving, putting one foot in front of the other. I had to remember the source from which this talk was coming. Everything that was said about me, if it didn't look like or sound like the words from my Father, I turned them around. If the words were, "You're broken," I would say, "I am whole." If the words sounded like, "You cannot make it without me," I turned them around too, stating, "I can do all things through Christ who gives me strength." My relationship with God grew stronger, and I was reminded of what God's love looked like. If my unequally yoked husband didn't mirror that, then I needed to go before the throne of grace to understand my place in a marriage that was never God-ordained.

As I mentioned earlier, when I met my husband, he was married. Of course, he told me his marriage was failing, but he was still married. What I accepted then was no longer acceptable. I knew I needed to release myself from this marriage in order to move forward. What became crystal clear was that God would never provide me with happiness at the hurt of someone else. He was still married. God would never send me a married man. If I were stronger in my faith, I never would have engaged with this man. He happened to fill a void in my life at that time. When that void was erased, I wondered what I was doing with him. We were not compatible in any way, and there was never the kind of love with him I needed, but I accepted the kind of love he was willing to offer so I didn't have to be alone. I could not have been more wrong.

As our court date grew closer, my pastor continued to instruct me to hire an attorney because my husband had a very experienced attorney and a host of military friends to come to court to vouch for his character and to talk about the kind of father he was, which was a joke. I, on the other hand, represented myself. God continued to tell me that I was not going to leave this divorce broken or broke. He reminded me of all the insurance policies he had already provided. I held on to that. I thought it was preposterous going to court on my own, but I felt confident I had done my research and had prepared for this day. I also served as my own attorney responding to his attorney through written documents. I would go to the law library and get samples of appropriate written responses and follow course. I actually became really good at it and found I loved that kind of research. I soon began to realize the energy I felt doing this kind of work would become the purpose for my pain.

When I arrived at court that day, I called my pastor to pray with me before I went in. I had my paperwork with me and a list of questions I wanted to ask. My husband and his attorney were already there, but there was another case ending, so we had to wait outside. I can still feel the energy I felt that morning. I was nervous, anxious, excitable, overwhelmed and a host of other things I just cannot describe. We went into the courtroom and the judge quickly came out afterwards. I sat to the left of this large room, and my husband and his attorney sat to the right. Soon after, one of my husband's military friends showed up. I was a little surprised because my husband never liked this guy, yet, he did what he thought he had to do to be successful in court. It didn't work.

My husband's attorney asked me questions on the stand, and there in my beautiful white pantsuit with navy blue pinstripes, I answered every single one without even blinking. Do not ask me from where this strength, this courage emanated. At the time, I didn't even think about it. I remember thinking at one point, "Wow, Lynn, that was good. You should remember that. How did you know to say that?" Oh yes, my two selves had conversations going like my friend, Ann and I on a Saturday creating another Lifetime movie moment. That moment was priceless.

Next up, attorney-thought-I-was asked her husband to approach. When he got on that stand, I ripped him to shreds to the degree that he nervously laughed and had the audacity to not want to answer my questions. I had fun with it. I said, "Your honor, could you please instruct the witness to answer the question." I got so tickled when the judge said, "Ma'am, he's not the witness, he is the plaintiff, but, yes, sir, answer the question." I got too big for my britches and spoke out of turn, but the judge knew what I meant.

His attorney asked the judge not to acknowledge the fact that my husband should have been paying child support. In the same breath, he asked the judge to honor the fact I signed away my rights to my husband's military retirement. The judge chided the attorney by saying he agreed with me because "you cannot pick and choose the parts of the binding separation agreement you like and ask to keep them and throw out the rest." I smiled and looked over at their table to the right of me and thought, "Take that, you Judge Advocate General (JAG) attorney with 20 years on me." It doesn't matter who he thought he was, nor did it matter how much experience he had because God doesn't call the qualified, He calls the inexperienced and qualifies them. And that is just what He did in the courtroom that day.

I won! I got exactly what I wanted, and it was a whole lot more than I ever could have imagined. And I divorced by representing myself against an experienced attorney and not paying exorbitant attorney fees. Additionally, I petitioned the court, and because he filed for divorce (at my request), I knew I could ask that he be remanded to pay my court costs, and the judge agreed. So, I received back child support, current child support for two years, furniture, my vehicle and my name. Yes, I knew that it would cost me nothing to return to my maiden name if I did so at court, as opposed to waiting afterwards. Even that shocked my husband. I had some nerve not wanting to keep his last name. Well, that's not the name my daddy gave me, and I wanted that name back. My maiden name represented a fresh start, and it represented for me the only man in my life who chose me for me, and even though he was not there to witness his little girl in the courtroom, I knew my daddy would have been so proud of me.

The divorce and everything that led up to it had taken a toll on my body. Once I got into my car, I sat there sobbing, alone with tears and screams of joy permeating the small space, but my left arm refused to raise up. I could only lift it halfway. I had developed frozen shoulder from the stress of it all and would go through months of physical therapy to heal from it. I still have trouble with my shoulder, and it is a reminder of the highs and lows of divorce. It is also a reminder of strength, tenacity, and perseverance in the wake of the storm that was divorce. I survived and thrived through it.

Throughout the process of my divorce, one thing was completely certain. It wasn't that it was this great epiphany, but it was the one thing that gave me solace, and it is that one of the most powerful lessons in life is the knowledge that we have control over one person and one person only: ourselves. I had to stop looking outside of myself to move forward because I knew that was a fruitless effort. I could not change anyone but myself, nor could I change anyone's perspective on Lynn. For a long time, I participated in a perception of a life that really was not mine. It was a fantasy for both my ex-husband and me. Well, it was time for me to turn and look inward and do the work on myself that would affect dramatic and positive change in my own life.

Being a victim means giving away all control and power. If I blamed someone else for my situation, then I realized I would be powerless to do anything about it, as that would be conceding to a choice to absolve myself of any responsibility for the decision and its' outcome.

I created change that would make my life better, but that could only truly happen if I stopped trying to change my ex or my current reality. I had to turn this entire situation over to God. He guided me through the divorce and now, I needed Him to guide me through the aftermath.

My God, the eraser of my guilty stain of divorce, reminded me in 1 Corinthians 7:15:

"But if the unbelieving partner separates, let it be so. In such cases the brother or sister is not enslaved. God has called you to peace."

I recall the day God released me from my marriage. I felt a sense of peace that is so unexplainable. I believe the grace that had been given to my husband to become the man God wanted him to be had run out. I was released to move forward, and that is exactly what I did.

Removal of the the Guilty Stain of Divorce

1. **A New Beginning** - I began thinking of my divorce as **new beginning** instead of a means to an end. Divorcing my husband was not a death sentence. I could begin again, but I had to really start believing that I could and that I was worthy of doing so. More than that, I had to start believing that someone else would find me **worthy**. The only problem was believing that myself. When I began to believe it, I really was able to see the personal growth that was a direct result of my divorce. There were so many challenges, and I believe there were more challenges than there were good times.

2. **Thanksgiving** - Still and all, every single time I see my daughter, especially as she is **growing** into her own, I am reminded this really was better than good. She was the good that was born out of that marriage, and I am **thankful** for that. She would often ask me, "If you don't think dad and you were ever supposed to be married, then why was I born?" It was a really good question, and I had to give it some thought. I believe my daughter was always supposed to be my daughter, but I believe my choice for her father was just that. I believe she was the good the Lord talks about when He says He will work all things out for the good of those that love Him. My daughter's father could very well have been someone else, but I quickly dismissed

116

that thought because despite their rocky relationship, my daughter loves her dad. I know she desires to have a life very different from the one she has with him today, but that is a story for another day. Perhaps another book?

3. **Positive Perspective** - A healthy dose of **positive perspective** was in order, and I had to take it as often as necessary. The defeating and self-limiting mindset would often creep up on me, and if I allowed myself to stay in that place, it was terribly difficult to let go of the weight of it. I found that it was so much easier to hold on to that mindset sometimes than it was to move forward thinking positively.

4. **Facing Reality** - Remember when I said I created a world, a life of fantasy because my reality was dismal compared to it? Here's where I really felt the sting of my reality and when I had to muster up those images of fantasy to help me cope. It was my mechanism of choice. Perhaps, it was not the healthiest, but I encourage you to find what works for you and stick with that thing until you can find the strength to move forward in a much healthier way. There is no magic pill or book of instructions to show you the way. It is all about you and you and you. I never wanted nor did I expect my life to be easy, nothing good ever is. I just didn't want it to be so hard. When you're going

through the healing process (man, is it a process), it is so very important to remind yourself to gain perspective regularly.

5. **Learning to Create** - Think of your situation in the grand scheme of things. What were the positive aspects of the marriage that you can attach yourself to that felt really good at the time? Well, create something that will help you to keep your thoughts realistic and honest. I had to recall other times when I felt so low and remember how God pulled me from those low points, like when I was molested. I wanted to remember how I felt about being molested then and measure that against how I felt about it in that moment. It allowed me to remember when it felt so bad and experience this present moment when it doesn't feel so bad at all. Now, I have moved past my pain to share in the pain of others like me. Sure, I have my moments when I question "why," but I know the "why" moments will never really go away. They may lessen, and the sting won't sting as much, but the reminders, though subtle, will always be there. I had to recognize that I have healed before and would do it again. This divorce was merely one of life's many peaks and troughs. Life goes on.

6. **Personal Growth** - Personal growth was a gift. Reflecting on my personal growth and all the things I

learned from my failed marriage was a large part of my healing. I would often reflect on the things I learned about myself. Things like what I wanted in my next partner, things I did not want, things I could compromise on and things that were non-negotiables. I found that my list of non-negotiables was not nearly as long as I always thought it to be and that the expectations for the things I didn't want weren't nearly as high as I thought. I found that I wasn't hard to live with or get along with at all. It is just that when you pick the person for you instead of God giving you that one person designed specifically for you, you find that the things you couldn't live with and the things you couldn't live without, are the things that we shine the light on most or focus on the most. I learned so much about other people and this world.

7. **Never giving up** - I learned that it is so easy to just give up. We turn our backs to the hard work in favor of what looks easy, only what looks easy is much harder than the things we gave up on. My husband was never to be mine. He belonged to someone else, but it looked easy and felt right in the midst of all the things I didn't have, so I went with it, even though my heart could never catch up to the act of me moving on without it. I had to remember who I was before I got married, or forget who I was because if engaging in a relationship with a married man was who I was, then

I needed to become someone different, not necessarily better, but wiser.

8. **Loving myself** - That woman wasn't perfect, but I liked her a lot better than I did the woman who married a man she was not in love with. That really wasn't fair to him, but I think we chose what looked right even though it didn't feel right. What positive things can you take from your experience that might be useful in the future? What things are possible now that weren't possible before? Have you changed in ways that you are proud of? Have you learned about a personal fault that you would like to grow past? Have you learned things about other people that will be useful in later relationships? I realized I must use my past relationships as a learning process and take that new knowledge and my personal growth into my future.

9. **Getting to know Lynn** - I had to **get to know Lynn** again. I looked familiar to myself, but sometimes I felt like a foreigner, an imposter. I lost a sense of myself because I was always giving and doing for others, never realizing that the more I gave, the more I would need. I was doing all the pouring, while no one bothered to pour. As scary as it was, I was looking forward to being on my own again. It wasn't as much of a shock as I thought it would be. Once again, I had

only myself to rely on in a world where it seemed everybody had somebody. I remembered how to be alone, and I didn't really stop to think if that was a good thing or a bad thing. I just adjusted and liked the adjustment... a lot.

10. **Not being boxed in** - Being in a relationship, especially a bad one, didn't define me. It occurred to me that I am and was whole with or without a man in my life. It's always hard to get into a new routine no matter what the circumstances behind it are, and it's normal to feel scared, confused, or listless in these situations. I began to focus on the things I loved and started remembering who I was on my own. I stopped beating myself up because of failures in my past. They didn't define me as a woman, a mother, a sister or a friend. Sometimes I got it right and at other times, I failed miserably, but the next time out the gate, I found success. I couldn't know success without failing first and failing forward.

11. **Letting my hair down** - I allowed myself some time to **be single** and didn't dive headfirst into another relationship. I learned how to be on my own, to become independent from another human being and tested my new walking legs. They held me up well, and I learned I liked the independence they brought me. Those legs were mine, not prosthetics,

but mine. I discovered new things and rediscovered old things, things I didn't know I liked, like sushi or convertibles or waking up at 3:00 a.m. to go to the gym or to write or read or riding ATVs on country roads. Those things were masked beautifully in my need to please others, hoping love would be my prize. I've learned **I am the prize, and love is the bonus**. I listened to music, all kinds and realized I wasn't stuck in one genre, but I thought I was because I settled into what someone else liked. I discovered how much I love art and how much I love my favorite team (for those of you who don't know, that would be the Dallas Cowboys). The world around me didn't seem so big. I summoned motivation to get acquainted and reacquainted with myself and began looking forward to my glorious future.

12. The great thing about my divorce is I didn't have to **learn to fall in love** because I already didn't know how. Truth be told, I was never in love my with ex-husband. Learning to love him was easy because that is a mandate by God that we love one another. That wasn't the only kind of love I expected in my marriage. I didn't like him all that much either, which sounds horrible, but it is my truth. I lived in a space, literally and figuratively, with a man I tolerated and hoped he wouldn't see me. I was okay with that, just as I was okay with him being with other women. We weren't

intimate, so it didn't matter to me. The choice to marry him, that mistake, was completely on me. I didn't get butterflies at the thought of him. No, not even from day one. I just wanted to be left alone, but since he persisted, I gave in.

13. **The aftermath** - After divorcing him, I contemplated **new relationships**, which seemed like unchartered territory, and I feared the unknown. Allowing myself to fall in love meant **taking a real risk**. To do it successfully, I would need to place a great amount of trust in another person, allowing that person to affect me, which would make me feel exposed and vulnerable. My defenses were challenged at the thought of it all. Because of my past experiences, the thought of being in another relationship caused me to be wary and to expect the worst. It felt like I was wired to recreate the past. However, with courage and persistence, I knew that love would eventually find me, and I could learn to trust again and restore my faith in true love.

14. **Rebuilding trust** - I was so thankful to God I had not become jaded by love, even though it felt so elusive and as if it had jaded me. Learning to **trust myself** and **developing self-love** would become an inner journey that involved examining my past from a fresh perspective. I had to believe I was good enough for

love and that a partner would choose me because he saw something in me that he just couldn't imagine being without and that no other woman could give him that "Lynn-thing" but *this* Lynn. This thought, along with a keen sense of humor, helped me to reclaim my life.

15. **Good enough** - I **accepted myself** and my life began to transform. I suddenly realized I didn't feel as dirty, that I had done the hard work to live and **breathe again**. The stains weren't as bright, and I really liked how the new red looked on me.

GS 6

The Stain of Isolation

"In isolation I ruthlessly plow the deep silences, seeking my opportunities like a miner seeking veins of treasures. In what shallow glimmering space shall I find what glimmering glory?"
~ Jamaica Kincaid

I sat alone with isolation for a very long time. We were glued at the hip. Proverbs 18:1 (MSG) says, "Loners who care only for themselves spit on the common good." Another translation (NKJV) says, "A man who isolates himself seeks his own desire; he rages against all wise judgment." I avoided social interaction due to the incessant guilt. I wallowed in social anxiety for fear of abandonment at even the thought of interacting socially for extended periods of time. My only contact was limited and superficial and necessary. Most of my contact was sterile. Sometimes isolation is a very good thing, being alone with your thoughts, reflecting on everything good in the world.

Temporal isolation could be the medicine that turns someone's life around completely, while long-term isolation can be the poison that takes away and destroys life. It can kill the spirit, warp the mind and taint the soul. All three of those evils had me in a stranglehold. Isolation, for me, was not the answer for my kids and me because I taught them how to isolate in an unhealthy way. They learned to discard everyone and anyone who didn't represent the picture they painted of them.

My daughter, especially, would make a new friend, and the moment that friend said something or did a very small thing she didn't like, she would dismiss the friend by saying the friend wasn't like her, so she had to let her go. Both of my kids became really good at being alone, until being alone felt like the only option, no longer a choice. They would isolate themselves and become angry or disheartened because they were alone, which was a choice in which they actively participated. This is when self-reflection and isolation become stains because often, the reflection in isolation doesn't appear as this beautiful picture with brilliant colors. Rather, the isolation appears as self-imposed walls, blurry with all color gone. Those walls become self-limiting, self-defeating, self-deprecating and self-loathing in many ways. The mind and the tongue can take you to the highest mountaintop or the lowest valley. In unhealthy isolation, it is usually the latter. Isolation was another blemish or blight against me because I felt I had harmed my children in a way that was, I thought, irreparable, and this caused even more damage to my view of self.

No, my children didn't appear to be scarred, and in reality, they weren't at all, but I couldn't see that. I believed anything my hands touched became dirty because I was dirty, unclean and damaged. Walking around with seemingly dirty hands was my doing because the energy of my soul was diminished by the molestation, betrayal, divorce, broken relationships and figuring out how to be a single mother, even when I was married. If I isolated, I could fantasize or ignore the pain, and people couldn't see the real me. I felt so much safer not allowing myself to feel anymore because then, there could be no more disappointments or hurt.

But I learned that not allowing myself to feel is a worse kind of pain than feeling and being hurt. The former showed humanity while the latter revealed a person a whisper away from oblivion. There is a quote by Winston Seeney that says, "Isolation can lead to uniqueness, but uniqueness also walks the halls of mental institutions." I knew that if I didn't integrate myself back into society that I would end up permanently etched into those walls and halls. My children deserved better.

Everyday became a day of positive affirmations. Everyday became a day where I had to remind myself to keep moving. When my feet stopped, there were days I had to pick them up with one hand and then the other until my brain finally clicked in. The motion of moving forward was just that on many occasions. There were no fluid motions, only robotic ones, at least in the beginning. Counseling was a welcome relief some days, and other days, it was another thing, another reminder of how much my soul had been tortured. The torment was everywhere—a word spoken by someone out of context; standing in line at the grocery store and smelling my stepfather's cologne or something vaguely similar; or a child laughing because I couldn't remember ever feeling that free as a little girl. Feeling sorry for myself was a badge of honor I wanted to uphold well... until I didn't. It was too exhausting. I was a prisoner of my own thoughts, and fighting to escape was liberating in some ways because it forced me to focus on something good.

I realized that no problem in my past would suddenly disappear and no problem exists in isolation. I began to reduce my isolation to its basic components, deconstructing them in a sense, and then reconstructing them and placing each component in its proper place. Drawing deeper into my own heart and mind allowed me to live in a world with less fear, less isolation and a lot less loneliness. Laughing genuinely became easier. I began meeting people who I have cherished like family. I began to see all the colors of the rainbow and appreciate each one. I began to see people as people, each with his or her own set of flaws. I became more understanding.

I learned the strength of forgiveness and how it has tentacles that spread far, wide and deep. Everyone needs to experience what it is like to forgive and to love deeply. I learned how to do both. I also realized that because my pain cut so deep, the wounds allowed love to go just as deep, unfiltered, not stymied nor hindered. But for love to penetrate, I had to open my heart again. I had to trust it and believe in it. I had to believe I was worth it. Once I found my voice, once I believed my worthiness, there was no stopping me. I developed a courage, a strength I no longer had to think about finding. It just happened. Something had awakened in me that was so pure and honest, I couldn't ignore it. I began to take risks in relationships, all kinds, and in love. I loved myself more than I could ever love another human being because that is how love is shared and known in the first place. Self-love is the most powerful resource there is. It is always at our disposal.

I often wonder when this new Lynn showed up. Who summoned her? Where was she hiding? Lynn showed up when she realized the beauty of her colors; when she realized no stain was too great; and when she realized the color red suited her. Character could not be created in isolation but by forging interactions and relationships with other people and the world. She began praying in earnest, daily, and believing God only wanted the best for her. He was waiting to give her the abundant life she so richly deserved. She was reminded it is so much easier to be a Christian in isolation than to step outside of the shadows and exercise her faith for the world to see, even when the world wanted nothing more than to crucify her. Yes, the world waited, but so did He, to remind them the stones they held may very well be used against them. Lynn was finally able to nod in agreement. There is a myriad of people who make up God's church. She wasn't the only imperfect Christian to show up on Sunday.

Removal of the Guilty Stain of Isolation

God, the eraser of my guilty stain of isolation, said there are times to isolate, which are good and necessary: *[1] "But understand this, that in the last days there will come times of difficulty. [2] For people will be lovers of self, lovers of money, proud, arrogant, abusive, disobedient to their parents, ungrateful, unholy, [3]heartless, unappeasable, slanderous, without self-control, brutal, not loving good, [4] treacherous, reckless, swollen with conceit, lovers of pleasure rather than lovers of God, [5] having the appearance of godliness, but denying its power. Avoid such people unto me." (2 Timothy 3:1-5)*

But there are still other times when isolating is not good for the soul: *"You shall not be partial in judgment. You shall hear the small and the great alike. You shall not be intimidated by anyone, for the judgment is God's. And the case that is too hard for you, you shall bring to me, and I will hear it."* (Deuternomy 1:17)

Here are the tools I used to prevent and combat isolation:

1. **Recognition** - I had to recognize it when it was near and then speak against it if it was healthy to do so. I recognized who my anchors were and drew close to them. They are my circle of grace and accountability.

2. **Affirmations** – I wrote words of affirmation to myself and read them daily. I was not one to do this before all

the darkness, but it has been a source of light in my life and has provided meaning and purpose to my being.

3. **Laughing** – Laughing seems easy enough, but when you extract it from your life as easily as you do people, you find there is no need to genuinely laugh, except at oneself. I started going to comedy shows often and watching hilarious movies. I learned not to take myself too seriously, which meant laughing at myself, a lot.

4. **Serving** – This was huge for me. I became an advocate for a domestic violence shelter and began to find opportunities in my community where I could serve God's people. When I volunteered at a homeless shelter for the first time, I cried at the humility and kindness from those I was serving. They taught me a very valuable lesson that day, one I have never forgotten. I have found that when we place our burdens at the altar and turn to help someone else in our darkest hour, that is where God shows up the greatest. And show up, did He.

This stain helped me to become completely and wholly Lynn. Really, this changes from day-to-day. No two days are the same. I am healing one day at a time, allowing myself to feel, to experience each gift that welcomes me, every moment. My voice allows me to breathe in those things that are life-giving while ignoring the rest.

"I now stop feeling guilty. I let myself out of that prison."

~ Louise Hay

GS 7

Completely Lynn

"With everything that has happened to you, you can either feel sorry for yourself or treat what has happened as a gift. Everything is either an opportunity to grow or an obstacle to keep you from growing. You get to choose."
~ Wayne W. Dyer

The number seven represents completion, so it was important for me to pen seven chapters in this book to represent how my life is becoming whole, and I am becoming "completely" Lynn.

Erasing those stains was not an easy feat, and quite honestly, they never really go away. Sure, they fade over time, but the faint outline is always a reminder of what was, what used to be, and how I was affected by the circumstances.

All too often, throughout my lifetime, I learned shame-based messages from my childhood that made their way into adulthood. Even the act of writing this book came with its messages of shame. Some wanted to shame me into not writing it because "it wasn't of God." I still wonder how those people know what my relationship is with God and what He spoke over my life. What I knew for sure was I had to keep moving, even if that meant moving alone.

Guilt and shame followed me around, coloring the way I saw the world. My desire to push the guilt away caused me to want to escape, tuck my tail and run and hide from hurtful emotions. I was always in fight or flight mode in response to the "danger" I felt from those difficult emotions.

Then one day, it all made sense. My pain had a purpose, and it was not to cast daily aspersions against myself, causing me to feel as if I was constantly going before the judge to face punishment. I began to recognize those emotional reactions and explored them more fully. I paid closer attention to the stories I told myself to explain my difficult emotions—stories like, someone else was to blame for how I feel, or I'm unworthy, etc. Someone else may have played a role for which I never asked them to audition, but I had the authority to rewrite the script and replace the cast. I began to do that, learning to separate truth from fiction, owning my own story and speaking truth to others.

I took what I learned about myself to alter how I engaged with others; to ultimately transform my life; to have more connection, creativity, and safety to be my authentic self. Self-awareness and compassion for others is the pathway that led me to this space because these twins helped me respond to situations with honesty and insight rather than fear and self-deprecation. The alternative really wasn't an option because that would mean ignoring what was happening inside of me, denying myself an important part of the human experience. This option served the perpetrators, and me even more, and would do more damage than my yesterday ever could.

As I was writing this book, I had a dream. When I awoke, I recall seeing myself on a stage speaking to a standing room only crowd. I was nervous at the thought, and the tears refused to stop. Public speaking was not my strong suit, or so I thought. That was before I found my voice and learned to use it. God opened doors for me to take public speaking classes, and after successfully completing those courses and having professors reach out and ask me to speak to subsequent groups and share my presentations, I realized I had a gift that I had been minimizing. I had boxed myself in for so long, I didn't realize what I was good at and areas where I needed help.

I often questioned why God allowed me to go through so much pain. I never wanted it easy, I just didn't want it to be so hard. I now realize my pain was like giving birth. I couldn't completely birth this spiritual child until it was ready to leave my womb. Now, my water has broken, and the child I've been carrying as a result of my pain is this body of work. If God had answered my prayers and stopped the pain, then He would have thwarted my destiny. My destiny is too great for me to be deprived of walking into it. I see that now. I see the vision now, so clearly, and I am grateful for every experience that has led me to this moment in time. I am eternally thankful.

I recall the story of Joseph and how he endured so much. Joseph was the most loved son of his father, Israel, and was given the famous "robe of many colors." That robe has so much symbolism, much like my own life that has so many colors etched into its fabric. When Joseph reported having dreams of his brothers, and even the stars and moon, bowing before him, their jealousy of Joseph grew. The brothers sold him into slavery. Even though God was with Joseph, Joseph still suffered majorly for many years until God elevated him to a position of great authority. God honors faithfulness and obedience.

I own my story, and though I am not defined by it, I also do not deny it. My journey has been long, arduous and difficult at times, but it has led to a more whole-hearted life. Most of us aren't consciously dishonest with ourselves; these defensive reactions largely happen below our awareness. We tend to disconnect from difficult emotions because we've been trained to discount them or because they are too painful to confront. But, the down side of ignoring our emotions and the stories they generate is not learning from them. And, that can cause you to be stuck in a maladaptive pattern of behavior, like lashing out at others, blaming them for your pain. I understood that this position would keep me chained to the past, barely able to breathe.

I carried the strong burden of guilt and shame of the past into present moments and brought fear and anxiety along to keep us all company. Fear and anxiety came along because there is an underlying fear connected to feelings of guilt. The shameful person in me feared being found out or exposed for my deep feelings towards myself, which is a completely invalid process, I know.

I continued to replay the emotional state associated with guilt believing I was unworthy of making peace with the past. Guilt and the conscious are synonymously tied. It is a misperception that there is a right or wrong course of action, and subsequently I found a connection to having performed a wrongful act in the past for which I should be punished, to include those wrongs committed against me. I believed that, even as a child, I should have been able to protect myself.

I felt like a scolded inner child unworthy of attaining inner peace. However, showing mercy towards myself, the way God had been merciful, was one of the greatest acts of kindness in the healing process to release the burden of the past. As I continue to journey through life and acquire a better understanding and awareness, I can now safely look back on the past with a feeling of a compassionate heart filled with forgiveness rather than guilt. I have learned to release the burden of carrying the guilt into the present moment for in doing so I not only heal the past, but simultaneously bring new life to the present and my future. My future self deserves that, and so does my past.

In a similar vein, shame is viewed as a product of failing to live up to an imagined ideal of oneself. I created an image of who I should be from a young age, which is the accumulation of the thoughts, fantasies and ideals of those whom I loved and respected, people who betrayed me. Unfortunately, those ideals no longer served me. So, I undertook a new life path and embarked upon a spiritual journey of self-discovery. It is a path that would transform me into a person who had a very clear and distinct voice. I began to articulate in a way that inspired and motivated others. I surprised myself because I felt I was weak (and still do sometimes) but knowing I could have such an impact on so many people took the focus off my wounds and battle scars and placed them squarely in perspective. My views changed at every angle.

Shame was once reflected in the ideals held by society because popular culture affirms a set of principles and conduct one must conform to if they are to be deemed worthy within the context of the established tribes. There are a set of do's and don'ts which are typically acquired in adolescence and this is no more evident within the context of marriage. Marriage and family are viewed as natural developments into adulthood for the young male and female. While there is some merit in being a virtuous citizen, upholding morale places restrictions that do not serve those who fall out of the bounds of these obligations. Thusly, when we fall, society only remembers the fall, not the climb. If the climb is remembered, there is always a remembrance or caveat to the fall. One never really escapes it. That is much how I felt after my many falls.

Shame had created an unrealistic measure of self-worth, since you create a point of separation between who you think you should be and who you actually are. This created the basis for my shame since I felt unworthy of measuring up to the image perpetuated in my mind. I accepted this thought process was merely a mirage, a canvas created by my mind in which I attempted to attain. There was a divide between my imagined self and the proposed self, the self of my fantasies, I suppose.

Masking my true emotions to appear normal did little to hide the truth because when my emotions ruptured and overwhelmed me, I either erupted or isolated, neither of which was a healthy choice.

Awareness of the guilt I harbored, and the self-loathing opened the gateway to the next healing doorway. There was a willingness to accept my internal state rather than oppose it, embracing the shame rather than running away from it or disowning it. Expressing myself became the final doorway to the healing process, since I needed to share and explore my feelings with others or a trained therapist in order to connect with my emotions at a deeper level and to subsequently transform them into empowering ones.

There is a spiritual message contained within the experience of guilt. Namely, guilt and shame obscure the real and authentic self waiting to emerge from behind the veil of cynicism and pride. My life has been a lot like a bow and arrow. I never used to hit my target just right because I had to pull the bow back and let go just right. It would hurt my fingers, so I became fearful of drawing back. I didn't want to feel the pain of it. Then, my perspective changed about the arrow.

Becoming *Completely Lynn*

Some may question what this means. If you think about it, when you break something, you must put it back together or the pieces never become whole again. I was broken and had been for some time. I remember one Saturday speaking with one of my paternal aunts about this book and the nature of it. I explained to her how some of my maternal family members had basically turned their backs to the truth and refused to support my effort. While I understand their choice not to support it, I just couldn't understand how they could protect the evil that had occurred. Then, it hit me. They aren't essentially protecting the evil, they are protecting their participation in it because to face the nasty truth means looking into a mirror. They aren't ready to do the work. My aunt reminded me to go forth because the truth sets captives free. Lies hold us captive. That was sound and profound advice, and it propelled me forward to finish the good work I began so long ago.

My aunt's advice and the following tools helped me to become completely Lynn. Oh no, I will never be complete as long as I breathe, but this dark chapter of my life is over as soon as my pen finishes the last stroke of the letter. It is finished.

1. **Commit** – I committed to deconstructing what wasn't working in my life and reconstructing it in my own truth.

2. **Pull Myself Together** – I remembered who I am, who I was meant to be, and my better days are ahead, not behind me.

3. **New Behaviors** - I realized I needed no validation from anyone to live my best life. I began to live for the first time in my life.

4. **No Voids Here** – I no longer look for or accept relationships with people to fill voids in my life, nor do I want to be that for someone else.

When life begins to drag me back with difficulties and memories of guilty stains like that arrow, I envision myself as the arrow being pulled back as far as I can go and then being launched much further than I could ever dream as a little girl sitting on the edge of her bed, just dreaming, hoping, yearning. Being pulled backward is not necessarily a bad thing because it has no choice but to launch me into something great. My stains are no longer associated with guilt. They color me beautiful!

So, I remain focused and keep aiming high, knowing that at the right angle and at just the right time, I'll land dead on center, completely transformed and becoming Lynn, the very best version of the wide-eyed little girl who knew not where her stains would take her. We made it, little girl, with a few more strokes to go. We can do it, together, hand-in-hand. And when it looks like the stains are becoming too vivid, our Father is waiting, arms open wide and an eraser or two always in hand. He knew us before we knew us, and He is smiling at who we are becoming... *completely Lynn*.

"It has always seemed that a fear of judgment is the mark of GUILT and the burden of insecurity."

~ Criss Jami

EPILOGUE

Guilt usually comes from a sense that we've done something wrong, either intentionally or accidentally, or that we've neglected to do something. It causes us to cower in corners. Sometimes guilt creates a sense that we've failed to fulfill an obligation or to live up to a responsibility or an expectation. Guilt drains us of energy. Let it go because it will eventually draw us back to the same behaviors of the past. There is no escaping the past if we continue to drag the old baggage with us. Although some of it has its place, we can do nothing with the rest, but we hold on for dear life anyway.

God has shown me a love that I could not have known otherwise. That feels like an awesome responsibility in and of itself. Has it been difficult? Yes! Have there been a trial or two I thought I could never surpass? Absolutely! What He has also shown me is that in the midst of it all, He's not only there, but He shows up with that plan He always talks about that is designed just for you and me. Life, choices and consequences do catch up with us to remind us that we have them; they exist. They also remind us that if we aren't careful, they come back in different ways.

There are also the choices that are made for us, decisions that affect our lives forever, but for which we had no control. They show up just as powerful and sometimes, even more so. Sometimes they are the culprits that do the most damage. Those decisions hurt most or at least they do and have for me. I am not minimizing my own choices, but I am giving myself a much-needed break from all the ridicule, oppression and turmoil I have inflicted upon myself. Not a pass, just a break from it all.

Between the pages of this book, I discuss the pain of identifying the root of the guilt and shame I felt after being molested, having a child as a single mother, being betrayed by my mother, dealing with broken relationships and overcoming divorce. I had to decide how I wanted to move forward and erase those stains that were causing me to remain stuck for so long after experiencing the trauma. I learned to retrain my thought process so that I no longer owned things for which I had no control over, like other people's actions.

Finding my own way was not an easy feat. I continued to focus on the things that happened to me, like being molested by my stepfather, my mother having an affair with my husband, teenage pregnancy and the list goes on. I realized this road was just too narrow to travel alone, so I sought therapy to help me combat the demons that were waiting for me every morning as I awoke. They were there mocking me, following me around day in and day out, reminding me that I was not, nor would I ever be good enough. I believed them… until I didn't.

Even if you have never experienced the things I have, the lessons I learned to help me cope with life's difficulties are ones you and I share in any regard and on every level. The mind is a powerful weapon and can be used to elevate and promote you in ways you cannot imagine. But when your mind becomes your enemy, you must fight against all demonic forces that want to stop you. This book is a stark reminder that no matter the travails in this life, you are worth it, and you are worthy. I encourage you to read my story with the transparency it offers. When you have finished, start fighting, living and loving in your truth. Do not be ashamed of your battles, for every single one of us have our own crosses to bear. Yours may not look like mine, but bear it you must. I am counting on you to succeed. You are more than a conqueror, so act like it!

"The beauty of life is, while we cannot undo what is done, we can see it, understand it, learn from it and change so that every new moment is spent not in regret, GUILT, fear or anger but in wisdom, understanding and LOVE."

~ Jennifer Edwards

A Love Letter

Dear Little One:

Look up! Raise your head. I know it is hard, and I know the abuse has taken its toll. Do not be ashamed. Let go of the guilt. Be encouraged. I have seen who you will become. I see you strong. I see you inspiring others who have suffered your pain. You have grown into much more than the woman you thought you'd be.

Your dreams don't come close to who you've actually become. It's okay. In order to move forward, you must move. Sure, I have seen you fall a time or two, but you get up stronger. Pray. He remembers you and He sees you. Tell your story. Cry if you must. Those are cleansing tears. They help remove the pain of yesterday to move you into healing for tomorrow.

There is purpose in your pain, and you discover it. You understand the why of it all. Don't focus on the mess; focus on the message. There is a story there, and people need to hear it. This life is your big stage. It is time for elevation, but you cannot go higher if you never take the stage. Make

151

your debut so you can take a bow at the end. The world is waiting to hear your voice.

You are more than enough. You are much greater than your mistakes. Leave yesterday behind as the pathway that has led you into today. Be drawn to the light, wherever it is found, even in the dark places. I know your path doesn't feel right. It actually hurts but hang on. Keep hoping. Keep dreaming. Keep loving. Your season is about to change. The Son is shining on you.

Some people will leave you, and still others will remain. Hold on to the ones who choose you, for the others are only there for a time. You will move through this life leaving marks on the world, and it will, in turn, leave marks on you. Embrace them all because they will be the marks and colors that make you the beautiful person you are.

You can always talk to me. We are one, and I will never leave you. Chin up, little one. We've got work to do.

Love,
Me

Acknowledgments

First and foremost, I thank my Lord and Savior, Jesus Christ for placing this book in my bosom in 2002. For 16 years, I ran from allowing this book to manifest because I told myself I couldn't do it due to the stigma that is associated with molestation and abuse. The weight of that stain, in particular, weighed me down and burdened me for many, many years. Yet, here I stand having completed the work, this work that my Father started in me so long ago. There is no pain without purpose and there is no purpose without pain. My pain led to the creation of this body of work. I wrote it out of my heart and am hoping and praying the words are not my own but those of my Father and they will speak through me to someone who really needs to be encouraged to erase the stains of molestation, betrayal, divorce, broken relationships and single motherhood. To God be the glory!

My beautiful children have rocked with me from day one of this life. They are beautiful souls, and I am so eternally grateful that I get to be the stewards over their lives. I am thankful that while my life has been difficult, these two human beings were not touched or impacted negatively. Even with the adversity, it has helped mold them and shape them into the people they are today. **Ra'Mon**, thank you for seeing in me what I could not have imagined for myself from the very beginning. You and I lived and loved through this life all on our own. It seemed all we had was each other. Yes, others were around, but we knew we could rely on each other. You for me and me for you. You purchased a book for me years ago about how to become a published author. Every time I would mention it, you would get happier than me. You would always say that my book was going to land me on Oprah because though the book wasn't even written, you understood the impact it would make on this world. You sat on the sidelines patiently waiting, knowing this moment would be. You knew that I was destined for this long before I could put that pen to paper. Thank you, baby boy!

Then came **Davida**. Baby girl, you have been a great source of support ever since you could barely walk. As you grew, you thought you were my protection, beating away anyone you thought meant me harm. You have been a fierce protector while allowing me to grow through this life with you. When you were born, I knew God was giving me you so that I could understand a mother's love and what it meant to protect her daughter, to fight for her with everything in me. Every time I thought about quitting and not continuing on this journey, you would be there telling me I must tell my truth and tell it in my own way. You are such a beautiful, old soul in a 22-year old body.

Ann, my dear friend, I met you when I moved to Virginia in May 2009. My life forever changed because I knew God gave me the friend I always needed. No judgments, no preconceived notions, just love, all love, all the time, no matter the weather. I had so much bottled up inside me. You offered a safe place in my storms to rest my head. You fed me, gave me shelter and sent me back out to live some more. I've called you in the middle of the night and early in the morning. There has never been a time when I can say you haven't been there, even coming over to my house at midnight with rain boots on, Daisy Dukes, a t-shirt and a shovel to help me kill a snake in the rain. That is a "true blue," friend. Thank you!

Shakeita, THANK YOU! Our friendship was formed in God's timing and in God's way. He knew exactly what I needed and when I needed it. If I call at 3:00 a.m., you answer. If I calll at 12:00 p.m., you answer the call in every way. You hear my heart and before you guide me, you are quick to tell me what God says. I cannot thank you enough for your sisterly love and unyielding support.

Part of this journey to writing my first book included starting my business and becoming an entrepreneur. **Rick**, I cannot thank you enough for guiding me through the process of becoming an entrepreneur, starting my own business, helping me market my book and getting it into the homes and on the bookshelves of people like me and those who serve as encouragers to people like me. You have been a great source of inspiration for me. I am truly thankful and grateful that you saw in me what I saw in you. Through the numerous hills and valleys, you were my mountaintop in so many ways.

To those of you who have stepped up and stepped out supporting me along this journey, your love and support helped get me through some very tough times. Life is meant to be done together. Many of you showed me that by taking this book on as if you had written it. You felt my pain and encouraged me to move forward in spite of it.

Finally, thank you to my family. While the majority of you did not and still do not support me writing this book and sharing it with the world, I hope and pray that it not only illuminated some of the darkness I felt (and still feel sometimes) in my world but that it also helped to shine a light into your own lives—a light that offers healing and hope towards a future that will shine brighter than the brightest stars. Unlocking arms with deceit and embracing the truth is both cathartic and liberating. Honoring the truth is meant to heal, only heal because anything else, especially hurt, is not genuine truth. Speaking truth to life and in life does not mean it won't hurt; it means only that it is a sincere and genuine attempt at clearing away the barriers and creating a blank space and time for healing. Healing is a process, and typically, there is nothing easy about it. Yet, there is something so beautiful and so pure about it when we allow ourselves to sift through it all, talk, create, laugh and just remember. It is my ultimate prayer that you will remember our better days are ahead, not behind; we are above and never beneath; we are the head and never the tail. I love you all and wish for each of you His very best and no less.

"You were never created to live depressed, defeated, GUILTY, condemned, ashamed or unworthy. You were created to be victorious."

~ Joel Osteen

A Note from the Author

As a Christian, I know that generational curses are real. Exodus 34:7 says that God "visits the iniquity of the fathers upon the children and the children's children to the third and fourth generation." These curses are not only sexual in nature but can be financial, spiritual, intellectual, emotional, etc. We all have "skeletons" in our proverbial closets. They weren't instilled in us by our mothers or fathers or grandmothers or aunts or uncles; they are actually the work of our first parents, Adam and Eve. We were in Adam when he transgressed God's commandment, and we were condemned along with him.

Unfortunately, my family has endured generational curses of sexual molestation and incest that have occurred from generation to generation and have not been acknowledged or addressed. Therefore, it almost becomes acceptable patterns of behavior where the resolution is to ignore that it occurred by just "moving on" and forgetting about it. This is nearly impossible, especially for the victim. For the victim, sexual molestation can be a very debilitating and dysfunctional event or series of events that can have longlasting effects on every single encounter or relationship that occurs after the defilement.

In order to remove the generational curses, we must be born into a whole new family tree (Romans 11:11-24). These curses are tied to choices, and for the lives of future generations to be changed, it can no longer be business as usual. Along the way, someone must take a stand and be steadfast in proclaiming the end to it. Satan must take notice that we are no longer blind to his attempts to kill, steal and destroy future generations.

I HAVE TAKEN THAT STAND IN PROCLAIMING IT IS OVER... the sexual molestation, the divorces, incest, poverty and lack... IT ENDS HERE!

About the Author

Calenthia Patrice Hall, or Lynn as she would become known, was born in Vero Beach, Florida to Dorothy Jean and Tommie Watson Hall, III. She is the middle child of eight siblings, three boys and five girls. Lynn is the proud mother of two adult-age children, Ra'Mon and Davida, who were very instrumental in Lynn meeting her destination of writing her first book.

Lynn began writing at a very early age and has kept journals in a cedar chest to mark her history, her life story. Her journey from there to here is marked with tragedy and triumph; from molestation to divorce and everything in between that bore the traits of a scarlet letter, guilty stains.

In 2002, God intervened and directed Lynn to begin writing her story. Though she would start and stop, this is the season that *is*, not the season that *was*, for the world to hear Lynn's story, Lynn's truth as only she can tell it.

You will be inspired by her optimism and honesty, her strength and courage, her resilience and tenacity to sojourn through life determined to meet her destiny. Lynn reminds you it is never too late to create your own terms and to live and breathe in them unapologetically.

CPSIA information can be obtained
at www.ICGtesting.com
Printed in the USA
BVHW092329201118
533618BV00021B/2000/P